Smile
Happiness Is Right Under Your Nose™

How the Power of Your Smile Connects You to Happiness, Love, Longevity and Much More

Mary Anne Puleio, Ph.D.

A **Smile Üp** Book

Published by Smile Up, LLC

Smile: Happiness Is Right Under Your Nose! How the Power of Your Smile Connects You to Happiness, Love, Longevity and Much More...Copyright © 2014 by Mary Anne Puleio, Ph.D. Printed and bound in the United States of America. All rights reserved.

No part of this book may be used or reproduced in any manner whatsoever without written permission from the author. While the author has made every effort to provide accurate information, telephone numbers, internet addresses, the author assumes no responsibility for errors. This includes any changes that may have occured after publication. Scanning, uploading, and distribution of this book via the internet or other means without the permission of the author is illegal and punishable by law. The material in this book is not meant to replace medical treatment, of any kind, without the advice of a physician. For information, please contact Smile Up, LLC, 3991 Gulf Shore Blvd. North, #301, Naples, FL 34103.

ISBN 978-0-9907211-1-6

ATTENTION CORPORATIONS, EDUCATIONAL INSTITUTIONS and PROFESSIONAL ORGANIZATIONS: Quantity discounts are available on bulk purchases of this book for educational or gift purchases. Special books or book excerpts can also be created by the author to fit specific needs. For information, please contact Smile Up, LLC, 3991 Gulf Shore Blvd. North, #301, Naples, FL 34103 or **visit the Smile Up, LLC website at: www.smileup.org.**

Smile
Happiness Is Right Under Your Nose™

How The Power Of Your Smile Connects You To
Happiness, Love, Longevity And Much More

Mary Anne Puleio, Ph.D.

Contents

1. Smiling and Purpose — 1
2. Smiling and Birth — 5
3. Smiling and Cooperation — 10
4. Smiling and Bonding — 15
5. Smiling and Health — 19
6. Smiling and Diet — 23
7. Smiling and Luck — 27
8. Smiling and Perception — 31
9. Smiling and Symbolism — 36
10. Smiling and Memory — 40
11. Smiling and Inner Peace — 44
12. Smiling and Endurance — 48
13. Smiling and First Impressions — 52
14. Smiling and Productivity — 56
15. Smiling and Beauty — 61

16.	Smiling and Rejection	65
17.	Smiling and Intimacy	69
18.	Smiling and Animals	74
19.	Smiling and Depression	78
20.	Smiling and Business	83
21.	Smiling and Social Networking	88
22.	Smiling and Judgment	92
23.	Smiling and Advertising	96
24.	Smiling and Renewable Resources	100
25.	Smiling and Culture	103
26.	Smiling and Contagion	108
27.	Smiling and Loneliness	112
28.	Smiling and Competence	116
29.	Smiling and Thought Control	119
30.	Smiling and Relationships	123
31.	Smiling and Self-Esteem	127
32.	Smiling and Education	131
33.	Smiling and Creativity	135
34.	Smiling and Income	139
35.	Smiling and Technology	143

36.	Smiling and Attitude	147
37.	Smiling and Leadership	151
38.	Smiling and Listening	156
39.	Smiling and Acknowledgment	160
40.	Smiling and Optimism	164
41.	Smiling and Sound	168
42.	Smiling and Play	172
43.	Smiling and Simplicity	176
44.	Smiling and Altruism	180
45.	Smiling and Longevity	183
46.	Smiling and Laughter	187
47.	Smiling and Inspiration	192
48.	Smiling and Forgiveness	195
49.	Smiling and Joy	200
50.	Smiling and Near Death Experience	204
51.	Smiling and Death	207
	NOTES	210
	Acknowledgments	227
	About the Author	229
	Other Books in the Smile Up Series	231

Smile: Happiness Is Right Under Your Nose!
— Mary Anne Puleio

Smiling and Purpose

Sometimes we just don't feel like smiling. Has anyone ever told you to smile when you don't want to? It can be very irritating. It can seem like an intrusion into your personal space.

As a child, I was constantly being told, "Just smile." I hated it. At five, I was diagnosed with a serious illness. As a result, I was frequently sick, and it didn't do much for my appearance or endurance. That's why my family kept telling me to smile—to put up a front as if everything was perfect. Honestly, the last thing I really wanted to do was hide the pain behind an insincere smile.

One day, I had had enough of feeling like an outcast. Determined to find some confidence despite my challenges I read *How to Win Friends and Influence People* by Dr. Dale Carnegie. After reading it, even as a child, I was convinced of the power of the smile. I knew, to turn my life around, I had to somehow find my genuine smile that Dr. Carnegie talked about so highly in his book. So how does a kid find their heartfelt smile, when it shouldn't have been lost in the first place?

In search of my smile, I created what I called my *happiness board*. I took a large piece of cardboard and drew lots of boxes on it. In each box, I placed something to remind me of things in my life that made me happy. A plastic, hot dog charm from a gumball machine would get glued in a box. It had the power to magically transport me to the sights, sounds and smells of Coney Island. Blissfully, I would be back at the ocean feeling the cool breezes, listening to the waves and savoring a vanilla cream soda—smiling.

My happiness board helped me to find my genuine smile. With a newly found smile, I learned to survive many challenges, such as the sudden death of my father, which left us homeless and living in poverty. As I began to smile more, I realized its incredible power. Indeed, just as Dr. Carnegie described it, my smile was infectious! When heartfelt and shared, it came with lots of opportunities.

Eventually, I created a multi-dimensional happiness model in my mind. This is where I store memories that conjure genuine smiles that are always at my disposal. Finding my inner smile has helped me to find my true beauty. It may sound corny, but finding my inner smile has also helped me to discover my life's purpose. Little did I know that as a child, I had already started creating this book on the smile.

Finding your heartfelt smile is powerful. Really, at the end of the day, don't we all just want to be happy and wish the same for others? The great thing about your genuine smile is that it will bring you happiness, and this feeling will spread to others. If that were not enough, the smile is free and it is contagious.

Humans are social animals. We all want to feel happy, but we also want to be accepted and have a sense of belonging. Our genuine smile connects us to people by letting them know we acknowledge them and that they are important to us. So as I work on my life's purpose, I'm smiling and I hope you will *catch* the feeling and smile too.

Smile Science—Who Knew?

Seeing a smile creates what scientists have termed the "halo" effect. The smile helps us to remember other happy events more vividly and to feel more optimistic, more positive and more motivated. The smile is also contagious and can help others *catch* the positive feelings associated with it. (Lewis and Edmonds 2005)

Smiling and Birth

Erin is considered a lucky baby. Born on July 7th at 7:00 a.m., she defied death and survived multiple heart and respiratory complications. After months of intensive care, Erin finally gets to go home. Her mommy, Lori, is thrilled but also scared to death. Erin is her first child. There are moments when Lori is plagued with self-doubt. She worries about her parenting skills.

That first night, Lori vigilantly watches over Erin. Out of the corner of her eye, she sees Erin's little toes peeking through her lace-fringed comforter. She gently covers Erin's incredibly tiny foot and wonders, "Will I be able to take care of this precious gift?"

The next morning, Lori breathes a sigh of relief. She cuddles Erin against her worried heart. And then it happens. Erin looks into her mommy's eyes and smiles. Suddenly, all Lori's doubts seem to vanish. She is filled with an indescribable joy. As if a switch were flipped, Lori's maternal instincts fire up when she sees that smile. She has a newly found confidence. Lori makes a silent vow, "Whatever it takes—I will forever find a way to protect my little girl from life's challenges."

Smile Magic—What's Happening?

Have you ever had a baby look you straight in the eye and flash their twinkling smile? Did it take your breath away? Some scientists call this neurological surge, *baby buzz*. It can happen in an instant. In that incredible moment you are filled with a rush of joy. Suddenly, you develop an insatiable need. You want to see that baby smile—again and again. Although it is flashed in a split second, the smile is irresistible and unforgettable. It has magical powers. It can forever change your life.

So what causes this powerful reaction? A baby's smile is actually addictive. When you see that special smile, it sends blood rushing to the pleasure center in your brain and you experience a surge of neurological changes. This sensation makes you feel very good. In fact, seeing the smile makes you feel so good it is compared to the pleasurable effects of some drugs or foods. It reinforces our maternal instincts. Incredibly, this response happens naturally when you see a baby smile—even when that baby is not your own child.

There is a profound theory that explains why our first smiles have this effect. It's because our smile developed as a survival mechanism. Think about it. When we are born we are totally dependent on the care and nurturing of others. Unable to speak, an infant's smile communicates for them. Raising a baby is hard work. Even the best of caretakers appreciate a little encouragement. Our first smiles speak straight to the heart of the receiver. They send an implicit message: "You're doing a good job. I love you, and please continue to take care of me."

No one has to teach a baby to smile. Scientists, using functional magnetic resonance imaging (fMRI) technology, have observed and captured photos of babies smiling in the womb one to two months before birth. When born, babies smile spontaneously in response to such things as a pleasant sound, a full tummy, or for no apparent reason.

Smile: Happiness Is Right Under Your Nose!

Once you are touched by the miracle of a baby's smile it leaves an indelible imprint on your heart. It can inspire you to love unconditionally. As some say, "You may have had the baby, but now the baby has you."

Smile Science—Who Knew?

Scientists used fMRI to scan the brains of mothers looking at photos of their babies smiling. The results revealed that seeing the smiling photos generated substantial brain activation in the reward centers of the mothers' brains. These are the same areas of the brain that are associated with pleasure and addiction. (Hrdy 2009)

Smiling and Cooperation

Josiah is strikingly handsome. He is 6'5", has jet-black hair and the physique of a professional football player. As he stands at the podium waiting for the award ceremony to begin, he is proud to be representing America.

When the national anthem is played, his heart aches with happiness and his eyes fill with tears. Years of dedication and hard work have finally paid off. His brother, a former NBA player, was usually the one in the limelight. Now it is his turn. Josiah is presented with the Olympic gold medal for the 100 meter race in track and field.

Although he can't see the audience, he can feel their excitement. His gratitude is undeniably expressed in his genuine smile. No one had to tell Josiah to smile. No one had to teach him to smile. Josiah is blind and has been since birth. His joy is a natural culmination of his feelings. His smile is an intrinsic expression of the joy upon realizing his dream at the Special Olympics in Beijing, China.

Smile Magic—What's Happening?

Surprisingly, even individuals born blind use different types of smiles to express their feelings. Why are they able to do this? Obviously, individuals born blind are unable to learn subtle smile differences by observation. Perhaps the answer is in our past.

Have you ever been in a situation where you smiled to be polite? Did you force yourself to smile because you didn't want to offend someone? If so, your smile was a nonverbal sign of cooperation.

Let's try an exercise. Close your eyes and back up thousands of years. Imagine yourself trying to survive during prehistoric times. Everywhere you turn there is danger. You can't even rest for a moment without fearing a woolly mammoth may step on you. Staying alive is tough.

You realize, teaming up with your fellow man would provide multiple benefits. Together, you would be able to combine resources. This would increase your odds of living.

So how do you make this happen? Showing some sign of cooperation would be helpful. Yet, how do you do this beyond the typical caveman grunt? You share your smile.

When you share your smile it connects you to others. Your smile helps others to feel acknowledged by you without speaking. You realize, when you share your smile it seems to make others feel comfortable and more trusting of you.

Even during prehistoric times, your smile is perceived by others as a sign of cooperation. Sharing your smile helps you to get accepted into the clan. Your smile enables you to stay alive because you don't have to attempt survival alone.

The simple smile is a complex communication tool. The smile is much more than just an expression of internal personal happiness. It also generates many outward messages.

Man actually has two smile pathways to the brain; one for conscious smiles and another for those that involuntarily slip past our lips. Either way, they are perceived by others to better

Smiling and Cooperation

interpret our intentions.

The smile is a powerful communication tool. It is one of the best ways to nonverbally express our need to show cooperation, acknowledgment, and acceptance of others.

Smile Science—Who Knew?

No one has to teach you to smile. Scientists analyzed more than 4,800 photographs of blind and sighted athletes who participated in Olympic competition. The results consistently revealed that both blind and sighted athletes smiled genuinely when they won, while the losers only smiled politely. It was clear that the losing athletes held back their feelings and pursed their lips to show a polite social smile. The winners' smiles were quite different. Their whole face lit up when they smiled, engaging the muscles around the mouth, cheeks and eyes—the signs of a genuine smile. This suggests that expressions like the smile are innate. (Matsumoto and Willingham 2009)

Smiling and Bonding

Have you ever had the kind of day that, despite your best efforts, everything you do goes wrong? Michael is having that kind of day. The deadline for his big project is fast approaching and the computer has crashed. If that isn't enough, clients are calling nonstop to complain about poor service. And then his company announces it is threatening to scale back budgets—again.

When Michael arrives home, he is depressed and overwhelmed. Exhausted from the challenges of the day, he collapses on the couch. While sitting there, his toddler, Claire, wobbles toward him and climbs into his lap. Uncanny as it may seem since she is just a baby, she intuitively senses that something is wrong with her daddy. Instinctively, she gives her father a big smile from ear to ear. Spontaneously, Michael smiles back at his little girl and like magic, he immediately feels better.

Do you ever try to hide your negative feelings from loved ones? This is what Michael was attempting to do, but his toddler was onto him. Remarkably, since she is only two, Claire was showing her daddy empathy. Although pint-sized—she is already prepackaged to relate to her father's feelings.

Smile Magic—What's Happening?

Babies actually come into the world hardwired and ready to smile. When we smile, at any age, it elicits an invitation to bond. Smiling creates an immediate, emotional connection with another person.

Besides bonding there's also another huge benefit of the shared smile. Within our brain are special cells called mirror neurons. These cells are activated when we observe other people's actions. This neurological system is amazing. It allows us to not only return the smile, but also to experience some of the same positive emotions as the sender of the original smile. This happens even if we feel terrible.

Smiling and Bonding

Smiling has big payoffs. Babies begin to realize this within months of birth. It entices attention. People will do almost anything to see a baby smile. Some people will start speaking in an unwritten foreign language—baby talk. Others may suddenly start exhibiting stunts from a Cirque du Soleil performance.

A baby's smile can also yield them some very pleasurable experiences, such as a soothing belly rub or a fun game of peek-a-boo. It doesn't take long for a baby to learn that this smile stuff is pretty powerful. They recognize that good things happen when they smile.

Smile Science—Who Knew?

We come into this world hardwired to smile. Scientists discovered that infants, even a few weeks after birth, can mimic an unfamiliar expression like the smile on a stranger's face. This is due to a system of brain cells called mirror neurons. Seeing someone smile triggers the same pathways to fire in the brain as if you were smiling yourself. Not only do you return the smile, but you also experience similar feelings related to the sender's smile. (Iacoboni, et al. 2008)

Smiling and Health

Max weighs in at 147 pounds and is about 2 years old. A regal, gentle giant, he is a Great Dane with floppy, triangular ears. Max participates in one of the thousands of pet therapy programs located throughout the world. Because of the many medical benefits associated with smiling, pet therapy uses animals to bring smiles to suffering patients. When Max trots by hospital rooms, it's difficult not to smile. People think they have seen a small horse. He stands over 6 feet tall on his hind legs. Max helps people smile during stressful health challenges.

Pet therapy programs carefully select animals to help bring genuine smiles to medically fragile children and adults. On a recent hospital visit, a loving Golden Retriever was placed in bed with a dying woman. The woman began stroking its fur and smiling. Her husband expressed with joy, "She has not smiled in two years." The woman died the next day, but her husband was filled with gratitude. He was moved to write a note to the program, thanking them for allowing him to see his wife smile one more time.

Sometimes a patient's fear or pain is so overwhelming that they feel they have no reason to smile again. Then a loving animal like Max can show up for a visit, and the smile that was lost is unexpectedly found again.

Smile Magic—What's Happening?

When you smile, it sets off a chain reaction. This produces a series of health benefits. As a result of that smile, *feel good* hormones are released while stress hormones are decreased. A smile boosts your immune system, the effectiveness of natural killer T cells and resistance to disease. Your smile also helps to decrease pain, accelerate healing and improve your mood.

There are so many health benefits associated with the smile; perhaps this is why centenarians list their ability to smile as one of their greatest life assets. Many believe that finding a reason to smile, no matter what life throws at you, has helped them survive for 100 plus years. Individuals that smile more in life statistically live longer and have more satisfying lives. Some doctors believe that frequently exhibiting positive emotions, like smiling, can also undo some of the negative damage caused by cardiovascular disease, psychological stress disorders and other chronic conditions.

It is difficult to comprehend how so much good can come from such a small gesture such as a gifted smile. The Children's Miracle Network Hospitals clearly recognize the healing power of the smile, and have set up the "Send a Smile" campaign. "Send a Smile" is a unique online social marketing project that allows users to create a free customized card via Facebook, Twitter, email or Pinterest. The card is then printed and delivered to one of the millions of ill children involved in the program to help bring a smile to them. Chico's is one company that has been deeply committed to helping with this worthwhile smile campaign and the Children's Miracle Network Hospitals. It has helped spread smiles to children throughout the Network's hospitals. (You can participate by going to: www.chicos.com/sendasmile)

Smile Science—Who Knew?

Smiling helps decrease pain and accelerate healing. Scientists found that when we smile, powerful hormones are released throughout our bodies. These hormones help boost the immune system and also improve our mood. The smile and its positive emotions can protect against poor health and help lower stress, a known risk factors for many diseases. (Ong, et al. 2011)

Smiling and Diet

One day I was sitting in the food court of my local shopping mall. A silver-haired senior, hunched over his walker, entered the scene. Slowly and methodically, he inched his way to his destination, the Dairy Queen counter. He ordered a vanilla ice cream cone.

Like a child, with ice cream dripping all over his face and hands—and not caring—he was ageless. His eyes were half closed as he savored the velvety treat. In his moment of ice cream bliss, time stood still. When he was done, he wiped his face. Slowly, he pulled his frail body back onto the walker, and started to inch himself away. As he passed me, we gave each other a knowing smile.

Smile Magic—What's Happening?

Do you remember your first ice cream cone? For many of us, food conjures up all sorts of smiles and happy memories. In fact, many of our favorite foods aren't so much about their flavor, but rather the unconscious memories we have associated with them. If you have a weight problem, you may want to consider stocking the fridge full of *smiles*.

Photos of yourself and smiling loved ones, placed on the refrigerator door, can intercept mindless eating. It's a type of mental reconditioning. The smiles in the photos connect you to something bigger in life than your waistline. Unconsciously, when you see the smiles and the positive memories they trigger, you are motivated to eat more conscientiously. The smiles feed your soul. They refocus your attention. They help you make smarter food choices.

Smile effects also boost your willpower. Still need some convincing? Consider this. In studies, people were asked to eat some unappealing foods. The distasteful morsels were found to be tastier, when individuals were unsuspectingly exposed

Smiling and Diet

to subliminal smiles before they began eating them. The smiles made the less-than-appetizing foods more appealing. More surprisingly, the participants didn't even know why.

Understanding why, when and what we eat is important. This knowledge is valuable and presents a recipe for smart eating. Even a vanilla ice cream cone is healthy with this formula. Capitalizing on this, the largest ice cream manufacturer in the world, Unilever, has come up with a way to have you associate your smile with the memory of their sweet treats. This manufacturer of favorites, like Ben and Jerry's, is placing ice cream booths in local malls throughout Europe. When you step into the booth, your picture is taken. No money is needed. The ice cream treat is yours free, but only if you smile!

Smile Science—Who Knew?

Boost your body image with smiles. Scientists from Maastricht University found that when individuals, concerned with their body weight, were greeted with a smiling face—it significantly lowered their anxiety about themselves. Also, the individual's confidence about their body satisfaction was raised after witnessing the smiles. (Martijn, et al. 2010)

Smiling and Luck

Smile and the odds are *lady luck* will smile back. Although some luck is random, most good fortune is a result of your state of mind. Many people believe that they make their own luck, and they would be right!

When I was in high school, I entered a public speaking competition and became a national finalist. Afterwards, when some people congratulated me they would add, "You're so lucky." Perhaps I was lucky, but consider this fact: less than a year before the competition, I was a stutterer and had been my whole life. Being a stutterer came with ridicule and teasing. It motivated me to find a way to stop.

As a strategy, I listened to recordings of John F. Kennedy's speeches. I found that when I would mouth the syllables of the words along with JFK, I could feel where and how they could emerge from me—smoothly. This process helped me to stop stuttering and boosted my confidence.

Secretly, I wanted the people who ridiculed me to respect me—so I entered the public speaking contest. At first, I was a nervous competitor, but soon developed a strategy. On the top and bottom of each page of my speeches I would write in really big letters: BREATHE and SMILE. I sensed that the judges appreciated my smile and it gave me a shot of confidence and a second to collect my thoughts. Lucky for me, my secret weapon was my smile!

Smile Magic—What's Happening?

Some people see every day as their lucky day. They approach life with a positive attitude and believe that misfortunes are actually opportunities waiting in disguise. Do you consider yourself a lucky person? If so, studies show that you also have an interesting trait—you're smiling frequently—at least twice as often as those that see themselves as unlucky. Lucky people know their smile is valuable, and they are not shy about exhibiting it.

How does the smile set you up for good fortune? Your smile

is an icebreaker. Like a social magnet, the smile invites people to connect with you. Research shows that people can pick up on another person's anxiety. Unfamiliar social situations can be stressful. When you smile it helps people feel comfortable and you come across more relaxed. It also lets others know you acknowledge them and want to know them. This increases your odds of creating lasting relationships and the benefits that accrue from having a wider social network.

Your smile is also a catalyst. When you smile, you get a boost of positive hormones that help to increase your self-esteem. Personality tests reveal that lucky individuals are less tense than the average person, and are able to express it in their smile. That shot of confidence you get from smiling can encourage you to take risks and try activities outside your comfort zone.

Also, your genuine smile puts you in that favorable light even with complete strangers. This is because studies have shown that people associate smiling individuals with people they think they already know.

Smile Science—Who Knew?

Smiling attracts luck. After studing lucky people for more than a decade, researchers found that the smile is like a social magnet. It gets you noticed, draws people to you and creates chance opportunities. Studies reveal that lucky people smile frequently—twice as much as those that consider themselves unlucky. (Wiseman 2003)

Smiling and Perception

When George Washington became the first president of the United States, he had only one natural tooth remaining in his mouth. As a child, he was ravaged with illnesses including smallpox. This left him with a lifetime of mouth problems.

At his inauguration in 1789, he was wearing his first set of dentures that were made of various animal materials such as hippopotamus bones. They had springs to help them open, and bolts to hold them together. He had to continuously bite down to keep his mouth closed. If he relaxed his jaw, his mouth would pop open.

Because of pain and disfigurement, it was difficult for Washington to smile naturally. For one of his official portraits, his mouth was actually stuffed with cotton to support his facial expression which produced a *forced* smile. Recently, forensic anthropologists performed laser scans on the remains of

Washington's dentures. The purpose was to develop a Smithsonian exhibit about the first president entitled, "A Leader's Smile."

Smile Magic—What's Happening?

George Washington's lifelong pain caused him to sometimes force a smile. Have you ever been in a social situation where you had to *fake* a smile? Did it feel uncomfortable? Perhaps you were turned off when you felt that someone had *insincerely* smiled at you? You are not alone. Phony smiles are a real turnoff for the majority of people. However, did you know that even a forced smile, in private, provides benefits back to you?

The next time you think you're feeling a bit down, try forcing a smile. Faking a smile can help change how you feel. How is this possible? It is because the forced smile can short circuit your perception of a bad mood.

Here's how the process works. When you feel sad, you're facial muscles automatically respond by frowning and putting on a sad face. This sends a message back to the brain, reinforcing

Smiling and Perception

that you feel unhappy. You can actually reverse this feedback loop by forcing yourself to smile which will send a different message back to your brain.

If necessary, do what some psychologists do with their patients involved in "Half-Smile Therapy." If needed, use something as simple as a pencil held horizontally between your teeth to force a smile. Hold the pencil in your mouth so it causes your cheeks to be raised and your eyes to be pinched. This is the facial expression of a sincere smile. Hold that position for at least 10 to 30 seconds.

Afterwards, pay attention to how you feel. Most people simply feel happier. This exercise is so easy you may think it cannot possibly put you in a better mood. Despite its simplicity, it does work. In fact, many severely depressed individuals have had such good results with regular smile therapy they have been able to cut back on antidepressant drugs.

This technique works because the brain does not differentiate between what is real and what we pretend to be real. Our facial expressions have the ability to affect how we feel—even if we are not *feeling* the emotion they are depicting. This is why individuals that have had botox injected into their facial muscles not only lessen their wrinkles, but also diminish their ability to feel certain emotions associated with these muscles.

When we use our muscles to produce even a fake smile, our brain recognizes a pathway that has become associated with happiness. The smile triggers a positive chain reaction. Even though the smile is forced, it still causes a release of healing and calming hormones throughout the body. The forced or fake smile is like a volume control on our perception of how we feel. As amazing and simple as it is, our forced smile helps us to personally tune up a more positive mood.

Smile Science—Who Knew?

Smiling helps lift your mood. Scientists asked participants to hold a pencil horizontally between their teeth. This action caused their cheeks to be raised and their eyes to be pinched which produces the same facial structure as a genuine smile. The participants consistently felt happier and rated a selection of cartoons funnier than those not forced to smile with the pencil. (Soussignan 2002)

Smiling and Symbolism

Have you ever seen those ads where someone famous is photographed with a milk mustache? Well, meet the newest smiley face, compliments of the dairy industry ☺. The electronic smiley face has morphed its way to stardom with a milk mustache makeover.

Harvey Ball created the first smiley face in 1963. The symbol was proposed to help boost employee morale at the State Mutual Assurance Company. Fearing that a grumpy employee would turn the smile upside down and into a frown, he added the eyes. In a project that took Harvey only minutes to create—smiley's have since been splashed across our eyes everywhere in the world for more than half a century.

The smiley face quickly became a universal symbol of happiness. More than 50 million smiley face buttons were sold in only one year in the 1970's. The symbol reached true fame when the

U.S. Post Office acknowledged its stardom and issued a smiley face stamp in the 1990's. Concerned about the over-commercialization of the image and a loss of its true intent, Harvey Ball proposed World Smile Day in 1999.

Now, each year on the first day of October, people from around the planet embody the theme, "Do an act of kindness. Help one person smile." Celebrating an international symbol of goodwill, thousands of charities have benefitted from fundraisers held on World Smile Day. Buttons with the words, "You've been smiled upon by the smiley" adorn the volunteers on this special day.

Smile Magic—What's Happening?

The smile, and all its symbolic variations, has a proven cash value. That's why consumers have also "been smiled upon by the smiley." Every day, people are exposed to thousands of commercial images from television ads and billboards to T-shirts and bumper stickers.

Every brand comes with a set of associations. Smiles capture our attention. They help put us in a good mood. That's why thousands of businesses have aligned themselves with a smiling image because of the happy feelings it provokes.

Pepsi is one of the latest companies to associate itself with the smile. In a $1.2 billion campaign, it is revamping its logo. The famed red-white-blue globe logo is being transformed into various "smiles" for its different products.

Not to be outdone by another soft drink giant, Coca-Cola has launched yet another happiness campaign. Coke products have a long history of identifying with the smile, such as "Have a Coke and a Smile." Now they have come up with the happiness vending machine to reinforce the association of your smile with their product.

Here's how it works. Unsuspecting consumers receive free gifts like flowers or a pizza when they nonchalantly go to buy a Coke from vending machines. Their exuberant smiles of surprise, as they receive the unexpected prizes, are captured via a camera on the machine. These encounters are inevitably posted on the internet. The winners quickly become international sensations, having a Coke and a smile!

Smile Science—Who Knew?

Smiles have cash value. Scientists exposed participants to subliminal smiles. Even though flashed for only 16 milliseconds (too short to register consciously) the participants were affected by the image. Individuals who had been exposed to the subliminal smile found the flavor of a so-so drink to be tastier and were willing to pay twice as much for the beverage than those who had not been exposed to the subliminal smile. (Berridge and Winkielman 2003)

Smiling and Memory

It's nearly 100 degrees outside and the soles of my sandals are melting into the pavement, but I am compelled. Just one more ride on Space Mountain and my day will be complete. I can hardly wait to feel the g-force as I rush down the coaster's biggest drop (you know the one where you have to make sure your glasses or hat don't fly off your head!).

I'm not the only one who has gotten caught up in the excitement of an amusement park like Walt Disney World. Just think of all the sainted parents that can't walk another step—and then find themselves eagerly waiting another hour to hear "It's a Small World" for the sake of their kids. And to think all this fun is forever captured in your smiling keepsake photo of the event!

Smile Magic—What's Happening?

Displaying smiling photos of loved ones or yourselves can have lasting and profound effects on your outlook and health. The smiles remembered from happy events help raise your confidence and optimism about life. Just looking at the photos trigger production of the hormone, oxytocin.

Once it is released, what does oxytocin do for you? Referred to as the *bonding hormone*, oxytocin helps you to make social attachments. Its chemical reaction lowers inhibitions. This makes it easier to bond and get closer to other people. It also helps us to recall these bonding experiences as happy memories.

Studies reveal that we don't get bored with happy memories like we do with material objects. When you reminisce about your life, what do you focus on? Most people choose to revisit positive memories. That's one reason we sometimes remember events through *rose-colored* glasses.

Perhaps you have been at a holiday gathering and somebody decides to take a group photo. Have you ever heard the words spoken before the shot is taken: "Okay, let's pretend we're having a good time and smile."

We like our memories happy. When you think about it, who really wants to display a photo of frowning people looking utterly miserable? Most people really are optimists at heart. That's why we prefer the smiling photos. The smiles help us frame or *reframe* events as happy memories.

Smile Science—Who Knew?

Scientists at Duke University found that people remember individuals more when those individuals smile. Recall of names was faster and more accurate, if they were associated with smiling faces. In addition, fMRI scans demonstrated that the participant's brains were more activated when viewing and recalling smiling faces rather than neutral faces. The head researchers proposed, "We are sensitive to people's positive signals like the smile because we want to remember people who were kind to us, in case we interact with them in the future." (Tsukiura and Cabeza 2011)

Smiling and Inner Peace

In the movie, *Eat Pray Love*, the main character, Elizabeth, searches the globe hoping to find the secret behind a satisfying life. After traveling halfway around the world, she believes that she will finally learn the answer from Ketut, a wise-old medicine man.

She's anxious and can't wait to hear the secret. She listens carefully and leans forward. Then Ketut shares the following wisdom, "Smile with face, smile with mind, even smile in liver." Ketut knows that when Elizabeth can smile with her whole body and spirit, she will find peace and acceptance of herself.

Smile Magic—What's Happening?

Have you ever given yourself a heartfelt smile? When you

find your inner smile, you envelop yourself in respect and love.

Do you know how to find your heartfelt smile? A good place to start is to conjure up some joyful thoughts. Think about what makes you happy? Your thoughts don't have to be complicated. A simple flower, a gentle breeze or the smiling face of someone you love might work; whatever makes you genuinely smile. When you feel the smile coming on try to capture the sensation.

Once you experience the feeling of your own loving smile, hold onto it and try practicing inner smile meditation. This is a discipline that has been taught by ancient cultures for centuries. In smile meditation, you extend the loving energy of your smile to every cell of your being. The Buddhist monk, Thích Nhất Hạnh, meditates with a smile and instructs others to do so. He shares, "Sometimes your joy is the source of your smile, but sometimes your smile can be the source of your joy."

Inner smile meditation puts you in the now. It is a means to bypass the ego and its relentless thought process. Begin the process with your found heartfelt smile and give it to yourself. Picture or think of the smile traveling throughout your entire being as you start your favorite form of meditation. Imagine your smile greeting every part of your body. You can start from your head and eventually end up at your toes.

You don't have to be a monk living in a cave to experience the benefits of this type of meditation. No special guru instruction is necessary. Amazingly, total body benefits start to accrue within minutes of beginning the meditation, without any special training. Smiling *within* during the mindfulness meditation practice provides numerous mental and physical benefits. These include physical relaxation, peacefulness and cognitive changes that will persist throughout the entire day—long after the smile meditation session.

Inner smile meditation can help bring serenity to yourself and to those around you. Our genuine smile which we find and give to ourselves is a loving elixir that envelops the core of our being in acceptance and peace.

Smile Science—Who Knew?

Inner smile mindfulness meditation can provide a source of peace and comfort in your life. Scientists at Wake Forest University found that participants with minimal meditation practice (one hour) dramatically reduced the experience of pain and pain-related brain activation. The meditation produced a 40% reduction in pain intensity and a 57% reduction in pain unpleasantness. The meditation produced a greater reduction in pain than even morphine or other pain-relieving drugs, which typically reduce pain by about 25%. (Zeidan, et al. 2011)

Smiling and Endurance

Russian Olympic weight trainers were able to significantly increase their endurance by simply smiling. Working with Charles Garfield, author of *Peak Performance*, the athletes were encouraged to smile instead of grimacing when they reached exhaustion during their training sessions. As a result, the athletes were able to add between 2 and 3 additional weight lifting repetitions to their strength and conditioning program.

Garfield was a strong believer in the power of tricking the mind into believing that one's body can handle more than it may think. In 1979 he met with sports psychologists and physiologists in Milan, Italy. The doctors challenged Garfield to lift 365 pounds despite the fact he had only been able to bench press 280 pounds during his recent training. Did he succeed? Yes. How was he able to lift the additional pounds on command? The doctors taught him to use his imagination and visualize himself successfully making the lift.

After that experience, Garfield began teaching others about the power we possess to influence our mind and the effect that it can have on athletic performance. He soon realized that by smiling, we can engage in a physical action that can force a positive mental reaction and increase endurance.

Smile Magic—What's Happening?

How were the Olympic athletes able to make such a significant change in their endurance when they thought they had reached their physical limitation? The athletes used their smile to trick their brains. Turns out the adage, "Grin and bear it", does have merit.

Your brain can't tell the difference between that which is real and that which you pretend is real. In other words, you can trick your mind to override what it believes to be your body's limitations. As a result, your smile influences your mental perception of how much physical and mental stress your body can handle.

Smile: Happiness Is Right Under Your Nose!

This is what happens from a physiological perspective when we smile. Even though we may believe we are pushed to our limit, by smiling our body will produce changes that allow us to increase both our mental and physical endurance. Smiling lowers our body's stress response and anxiety during periods of pressure. The physical act of smiling also influences our body's physical and mental reactions by producing hormones that relax muscles, improve respiration and reduce pain. Amazingly, this positive reaction occurs whether we feel like smiling or not.

———————— ————————

Smile Science—Who Knew?

Smiling increases our physical and mental strength. Scientists from the University of Kansas subjected participants to a series of activities designed to increase stress levels, such as plunging their hand into a bucket of ice cold water. Individuals who were forced to smile, while undergoing the stressful exercises, had better recovery heart rates than those with neutral faces. (Kraft and Pressman 2012)

Smiling and First Impressions

Years ago I had the opportunity to interview for a position in the information industry. As part of the process, I met with a panel of experts. Understandably, I was nervous as we started the evaluation.

During the interview, I referred to the president of the organization as Dick Richard. Unbeknownst to me his name was actually Richard Dick. As a quick recovery, I smiled and said, "Is there really any difference?" Everyone smiled and it definitely helped break the ice. And yes, eventually I landed the job—smiling!

Smile Magic—What's Happening?

People judge our personalities before we ever have a chance

to open our mouth to speak. It takes the average person less than one sixth of a second to recognize a facial expression. Within seconds of meeting you, people are unconsciously searching for your smile. Why do they do this? It's because the smile is important. Your smile makes people feel more comfortable and well received.

People equate sincere smiles with acceptance. Scientists have found that we form opinions of people within 3 seconds or less of meeting them. Smiles flashed in as little as four one thousandths of a second were found to influence a receiver's impression to feel more positive without them even knowing why.

As much as 75% of our opinion of others is influenced by their nonverbal behavior. It's not so much what you SAY, but what you DO, that can have the greatest impact during a first encounter. Whether right or wrong, a first impression never fully fades from our memory. When we walk away from a first impression we retain a mental snapshot—a head to toe image that we instantly develop and never completely forget. Your smile increases the odds of a positive first impression.

Smiles are also incredibly contagious and make an indelible

impact when we meet people for the first time. Have you ever been in a situation where you really didn't feel like smiling? Then you meet someone who has an infectious smile. You may still be in a lousy mood or saying to yourself, "I'm not going to smile." Then it happens anyway. You smile back at them. It's difficult not to return a genuine smile. The smile can break the ice and open a door that was shut tight.

Also, people prefer to be around optimists. Your smile puts you in that light. How would you feel if you met someone for the first time, and they continuously scowled at you? Despite attempts to rectify an early bad impression, it can permanently cripple a relationship. Sharing a smile is one of the best ways to make a positive impression.

Smile Science—Who Knew?

When making new acquaintances, even the subtlest of smiles or frowns play into our judgment of another person without our conscious awareness. Scientists have found that smiles are so important in creating favorable first impressions that people unconsciously search for your smile within the first seconds of meeting you. The smile lets you know that you will likely get a positive reception. (Ekman 2003)

Smiling and Productivity

Zappos is the #1 online shoe company in the world. If you are fortunate enough to secure an interview at Zappos, they may ask about your creative capabilities. In response, drawing a rainbow colored pig has proven to be a wise career move. That's because at this company, not only is your art work considered valuable, but the smiles generated by it are a corporate asset. Such unconventional thinking has consistently landed Zappos at the top of Fortune Magazine's "100 Best Places to Work" list.

Zappos cultivates and delivers smiles. Its company culture encourages fun at work mixed with a tad of weirdness and respect for individual diversity. This philosophy has been a winning formula for the business. They were recently acquired by Amazon for $1.2 billion.

Smile Magic—What's Happening?

Let's face it, when you believe that your input is important to a project you tend to be more motivated to work on it. Productivity has been found to be directly tied to employees' beliefs that their contributions are valuable and necessary to achieving the organization's end goals.

Creating an environment where employees are truly and naturally motivated results in happier workers with sustained smile power. And those positive feelings spread among employees and ultimately influence customers. It is estimated that the average person can spend as much as 80% of their waking time at work and at job related activities. These include hours spent on the job, getting ready for work, commuting to work and thinking about work.

Want a sure way to kill productivity at work? Create a tension-filled, inflexible work environment with overly strict management. Studies show that the most serious work environments tend to be the least productive. Unnecessary, stressful situations can obliterate creativity and reduce motivation and productivity.

Organized play has been found to foster employee bonding, job satisfaction, dedication and teamwork. In addition, studies show that even under stressful situations and the most difficult of challenges, sincere smiles shared amongst workers foster collaboration. Genuine smiles shared with coworkers have been found to encourage employees to reach goals more quickly and with fewer difficulties.

Building an infrastructure that supports a happiness culture is a key to increasing productivity and efficiency in business. Sometimes that means letting employees have some time and space to release stress, bond and develop mutual respect and appreciation for each other.

This is an area where Zappos really shines. Managers at the company are actually encouraged to spend time "goofing off" with other employees outside of work to reinforce its unconventional culture—and it works. Employees are more productive at work when they are content and have a true spirit of happiness and a natural inclination to smile. One Zappos customer service representative shared, "We're not just motivated we're inspired… I have higher self-confidence, I hold doors open for strangers and smile at them."

So much time is spent on the job or in job-related activities, it is not surprising that in addition to being more productive, smiling employees are also healthier and have greater satisfaction with their lives.

Smile Science—Who Knew?

Employees' smiles can improve an organization's bottom line. Scientists studied more than 3,000 respondents in 79 countries and found that happiness at work is closely correlated to greater performance and productivity as well as greater energy, better reviews, faster promotions, higher income, better health and increased satisfaction with life. The happiest smiling employees are 180% more energized than less content colleagues; 155% happier with their jobs; 150% happier with life; 50% more motivated; and 50% more productive. (Pryce-Jones 2010)

Smiling and Beauty

Terri is obsessed with her appearance. Each day her alarm clock goes off at 5:30 a.m. She spends nearly three hours getting ready to go to work. She meticulously applies her makeup and is a perfectionist about her designer clothes. She spends more than an hour getting her blond-highlighted hair to spike and fluff just right. Heaven forbid a high humidity day rolls around and she is cursed with a bad hair day. Terri has actually missed work when this tragedy falls upon her.

Terri doesn't realize it, but she has a major beauty problem. Although her colleagues appreciate her efforts, they talk behind her back about her appearance. Why? It's because Terri never smiles. Secretly her coworkers murmur, "If she would just smile, she would seem so much prettier."

On the flip side, Patti works in the same office. She is a carefree soul. She hasn't been blessed with the greatest of looks, but she is confident with who she is and what she's got. Although she spends a minimum amount of time on her appearance, everyone thinks she is very attractive. Why is this so? Because when Patti smiles it's so sincere it lights up the room. Instantly, her coworkers are drawn to her inner beauty.

It turns out, in a multi-billion dollar industry, the must have beauty secret of the season is free. It's our smile.

Smile Magic—What's Happening?

Are you one of those individuals who would never leave the house without your lipstick on or your hair in place? After reading this, you may want to change that regimen to never leaving the house without your smile on. Studies conducted worldwide have found that we perceive people to be more attractive when they smile.

Unfortunately most of us take our smile for granted. Do you? It surprises most people to learn that identical faces are rated as being more beautiful when seen with a smile than without.

Smiling and Beauty

Is this enough to convince you of the beauty benefits of your smile? If not, there's more compelling information. Not only are the smiling individuals perceived to be more beautiful, but they are also viewed as being more intelligent, kind and sociable. Remember the only difference in the individual is their smile.

Smile effects are not limited to adults. Smiling babies are also judged to be more beautiful and cuter than non-smiling infants. Consequently, they receive more attention. Even orphaned children are more likely to be adopted when they sport beautiful smiles.

Smile Science—Who Knew?

Smiling is your greatest beauty secret. Scientists in England discovered that our smile makes a significant difference in how others perceive our attractiveness. Studying more than 1,000 individuals the evidence was quite compelling. When shown photographs of the same women, more than 73% of the participants believed that smiling women without makeup were more attractive compared to women wearing makeup, but not smiling. Even identical faces were perceived to be more beautiful when witnessed with a smile. In addition, the smiling faces were also judged to be more interesting and less moody. (O'Doherty, et al. 2003)

Smiling and Rejection

Marcus' rejection smile went viral and gave new meaning to the phrase, "Snap out of it." Facing unemployment, Marcus was ripping up another rejection letter in front of his eight month old son, Micah. For some unknown reason, this sent the infant into fits of uncontrollable laughter, lasting as long as two minutes. After capturing the moment on video, Micah's belly outburst of happiness over the rejection letter made it onto YouTube.

The video of Micah's smiles and laughter quickly spread with help from people like actress Alyssa Milano. She posted a link to the video and tweeted, "If this doesn't make you smile, check your pulse."

With more than 5.5 million views of the video, little Micah became an overnight sensation. Father Marcus was still out of work, but baby Micah's laughs were being marketed as a ringtone for 99 cents a pop and both were experiencing the sweet smile of rejection!

Smile Magic—What's Happening?

Unfortunately, not all rejection encounters end on such a happy note. If you've been through the heartbreak of rejection, you know how hard it is to recover. Exclusion hurts. Desperate to find an answer, we look for someone to blame and usually it starts with ourselves. Have you ever been a victim of, "I can't do anything right" syndrome? Whatever the circumstances, rejection is difficult and its resulting pain is very real. Rebounding is tough. It's easy to fall into a pattern of social avoidance and negative thinking.

How do you help someone or yourself if you have been socially rejected? Ironically, the only way to heal from social rejection is to trust and have faith in people again. After being rejected we become hypersensitive to all nonverbal expressions of acceptance or disapproval such as smiles and frowns. It's a defense mechanism.

Smiling and Rejection

Our smile plays a crucial role in recovering from rejection because people perceive the genuine smile as the most reliable expression of acceptance. Also, smiling or seeing a smile causes an immediate release of *feel good* hormones such as serotonin which raises confidence.

Do you know someone who is experiencing the pain of rejection? If so, consider sharing a heartfelt smile with them. Scientists using fMRI technology found that social rejection hurts so badly it actually activates the same area of the brain as physical pain. Your sincere smile can literally soothe the rejected soul and help to heal it.

Smile Science—Who Knew?

Scientists from the University of Kentucky and Florida State University discovered, after studying hundreds of adults, that individuals who had been socially rejected were more drawn to people who demonstrated genuine smiles. This is because rejected individuals perceive the genuine smile as the most reliable nonverbal sign of social acceptance. (DeWall, Maner and Rouby 2009)

Smiling and Intimacy

Jess is a real sex magnet, but when she really wants to attract her lover, she puckers-up and smiles.

She and Matt, her husband, have been married for 17 years. They are a passionate couple. Jess is demanding and sometimes Matt momentarily thinks to himself, "This woman is going to be the death of me!" But even after an intense argument, Jess can smile that smile at Matt. The smile stops him in his tracks. It melts his heart. His defenses disappear. Strangely, these passionate episodes just seem to bring the two of them even closer together.

Smiles can have many messages—one of which is love. From the beginning of time, poets, painters and sculptors have tried to depict the allure of a lover's smile. Even the most gifted of artists have struggled with this one! This is because it's not easy to put the silent and intangible smile into words or on canvas.

Perhaps the most famous artist to undertake the task was Leonardo Da Vinci. He spent years working on capturing the smile of the Mona Lisa. Though the actual finished work is relatively small—only 30x20 inches—it is believed to have been his favorite work and it was difficult for him to part with it after its completion. Was Da Vinci infatuated with her smile? Some critics speculate that she was silently communicating, "Come, taste the forbidden fruit" with that upturned smile. What do you think?

Smile Magic—What's Happening?

When we are sexually excited, the lips swell and redden. A plump, red smile is an invitation for intimacy. That's why the Egyptians used strong red wines to dye their lips to attract their lovers.

Science reveals that smile benefits are more profound than we first realized. Evidence shows that smiles provide an oxytocin boost when we see them. Oxytocin is known as the love and bonding hormone. It is also associated with pleasure and trust. When oxytocin is released within our bodies it helps us to make intimate connections and attachments. Just thinking of a lover's smile can trigger oxytocin and a chemical reaction that biologically attracts us to our partner.

The research on oxytocin is so far reaching it is being studied as an antidote for infidelity. When levels of oxytocin production are increased, partners have been found to have a pronounced desire to smile and lovingly gaze longer at each other. Personal attachment and sexual arousal is also heightened. Synthesized oxytocin nasal spray is being developed to help raise the hormone in people who have naturally low levels. The hope is the spray will help them to be more comfortable bonding and creating trusting relationships.

Studying the *love-struck* comes with challenges. Lovers seem to have their own unwritten language. When you're in love, it is actually difficult not to think of your lover and their endearing smile. Researchers found that love, like other strong emotions, comes with its own set of nonverbal behaviors. When asked to recall and describe their lovers, participants frequently responded nonverbally. In the language of love, the respondents simply leaned forward in silence and smiled.

So, do you realize the impact of your intimate smile? The composition and shape of your smile can be irresistible to your lover. It can also be relentlessly unforgettable. Not surprisingly, the smile is most frequently identified as a partner's most beautiful physical asset.

Smile Science—Who Knew?

The smile is a powerful and intimate gesture of emotion. German scientists found that women smiled more in accordance with their reproductive cycles. The studies reveal that women's smiles are more pronounced and frequent, in response to images of men, during the most fertile period of their monthly cycles. (Mass, et al. 2009)

Smiling and Animals

Wherever Molly goes she leaves a smile behind. Molly has a smiley face imprinted on the bottom of her prosthetic leg. The smile is a symbol of the joy she inspires in others. After hurricane Katrina, Molly was homeless and viciously attacked. Refusing to give up and die, Molly, a gray-speckled pony, eventually found a new home.

Molly's proud new owner explains that this horse has no ordinary farm life. She spends her days visiting the sick and elderly, is the subject of a children's book, and appears regularly on television. She's an inspiration. The smiley face on the bottom of her artificial hoof is a symbol. Its imprint marks a trail of happiness as a reminder to all who follow in her path.

Smile Magic—What's Happening?

People love their pets. They bring authentic smiles to our lives. Besides their zany antics, some believe that they understand and love us unconditionally—perhaps better than our human counterparts. Have you ever been comforted by an animal when you were sick? If so, you know how perceptive they can be to our needs. We can be at our absolute worst, and even the most finicky of pets can sense our pain and comfort us. Gingerly, they may lay their head on us while lovingly looking into our eyes as if to say, "I know you're hurting. Everything is going to be okay."

If you've ever had this type of encounter with your pet, then, inevitably, you consider it to be a member of your family. A recent study revealed that 7 out 10 dog owners viewed their animal as a family member and not just a pet. Some people wouldn't dream of taking a family photo without including their loving pet in it. Our furry friends truly make us smile. But, have you ever felt like your pet is smiling back at you? If so, you're definitely not alone and you're not crazy.

Animals do change their facial muscles to express emotion.

And if that weren't enough, now there is evidence that our pooch is also reading our facial expressions and can recognize whether or not we are smiling back at them. Most pet owners could have told you that already!

---------- ----------

Smile Science—Who Knew?

Japanese scientists were able to show there may be truth to the perception that animals express and understand emotions. Researchers studied the behavior of Labrador retrievers and Standard poodles while being put through a short training course. While going through a maze, the dogs consistently reacted to and recognized smiling faces, versus neutral and angry expressions. This supports the theory that the animals have social and visual cognitive capabilities. (Nagasawa, et al. 2011)

Smiling and Depression

Roger that, Mission Smile has landed. How much astronauts smile under adversity can predict how well they will do in outer space. Astronauts can live for months without sunlight, and in close quarters with the same people. These adverse conditions can often lead to depression.

Depression can impair judgment. It can cause a critical error. That's why astronauts are being trained to intercept depression by monitoring their smile frequency. Deep on the ocean floor in an underwater lab that mimics a space station, technology continuously measures the astronauts' facial expressions.

As soon as it is observed that an astronaut's smile rate has dropped, they are instructed to immediately engage in behavior that counteracts depression. The strategies aren't complicated and can be as easy as viewing a photo of a smiling loved one or enjoying a simple cup of coffee. The key is that the tactics are quickly applied to get them smiling again and back on a positive track. On Planet Earth, and in outer space, a happy astronaut is a smiling astronaut.

Smile Magic—What's Happening?

Would you want to be on a mission in outer space with a depressed astronaut? Most people wouldn't even want to be on a flight from New York to California with a severely depressed pilot or crew. That's one reason airlines have made it a routine practice to have employees warmly greet passengers with a smile as they enter the plane.

What's fascinating about this space scenario is that, given all the sophisticated technology, it is the simple smile that is used as a gauge to monitor and change an astronaut's mood. That's how powerful the effects of our smile are on our well-being.

You may not be able to eliminate depressive moods, but you can certainly take a proactive approach to them. You can do this by monitoring your smile frequency. If you are starting to plummet into a dark mood, force yourself to smile. Remember this doesn't have to be a complicated process. In fact, the reality is that it is incredibly simple. Think about or engage in some activity that makes you smile.

Sometimes something as simple as a soothing cup of tea or listening to some favorite music can do the trick. If all else fails, you can even force yourself to smile by firmly placing a pencil or pen in your mouth horizontally. This will cause your cheeks to rise and your eyes to be pinched—the position of the genuine smile. It doesn't matter whether you feel happy or not, it still produces positive results.

Even when your smile is forced it will release mind-boosting endorphins and increase your serotonin levels. Modulating our facial muscles from a frown to a smile sends a message to our brain that short circuits depression. The smile tricks the brain into thinking it is happy.

What wires together, fires together. In other words, facial expressions like the smile have the ability to positively affect our mindset. Conversely, by frowning you can bring on a bad mood. Still skeptical, that your smile can be this powerful? That's because it's such an easy concept. Sometimes it's the simple things that can be the hardest to believe, but the most valuable.

Smile Science—Who Knew?

The inability to smile elevates depression. Scientists at the University of Pittsburgh found that individuals, who could not physically smile, were not able to adequately express positive emotion. This reduced positive feedback they might have received from smiling, leading to a loss of social connections and an increase in depression. (VanSwearingen and Cohn 2005)

Smiling and Business

Thousands of passengers race through Tokyo's high speed rail stations each day. Now, riders may be guaranteed a smoother ride by some smiling employees. A Japanese railway company has installed *smile scanners* at 15 of their network's stations. The purpose is to encourage employees to start their day off smiling, under the premise that the resulting cheer will spread and increase customer satisfaction.

Each morning, the railway's employees can choose to enhance their mood with suggestions from the smile scanner. After having their smile evaluated by the scanner's software on a 0% to 100% scale—advice is provided. Based on feedback from eye and mouth muscle movement and lip curvature, employees with low scores receive messages like, "You look too serious, lift up your mouth corners." Using sophisticated algorithms, the smile's authenticity can now be quantified without the ambiguities of verbal labels. Perhaps Leonardo Da Vinci's famed Mona Lisa could have also benefited from the same measurement techniques. Scientists have calculated that Mona's smile is: "83% happy, 9% disgusted, 6% fearful and 2% angry!"

Smile Magic—What's Happening?

Splitting the smile into its smallest denominator to determine genuineness is extreme, but to many businesses the smile is synonymous with increased revenue and customer satisfaction. Studies repeatedly show that when customers encounter smiling employees, even when the smiles are intentional, they return to those businesses more often and buy more. In addition, consumers are more likely to remember the encounter positively and recommend the business to others. Conversely, a primary reason consumers express that they switch from one business to another is rude or unpleasant service encounters.

The evidence is clear: smiles have proven cash value. So how does a business encourage its staff to be upbeat and to provide service with a smile? Some companies try to seek out and hire people who are inclined to smile naturally. Holiday Inn has used a smile measurement system during interviews. Job applicants who did not smile at least four times during the interview were automatically eliminated. Greyhound Lines has also used a similar test. Customer service applicants who did not smile at least five times during a fifteen minute interview could not be hired.

Some companies rely heavily on smile training. George Washington University Hospital in the District of Columbia trained all hospital employees in quality customer procedures. At the end of the training, all 1,700 employees were required to sign a pledge to uphold the learned strategies which included greeting all people with a smile. Failure to do so could result in termination.

And then there is Disney. Perhaps there is no other company that is more invested in the smile factor. In the global world of Disney's success, "smiling is elevated to a philosophy of work and life." Disney employees go through extensive smile training. Why are they so committed to the art of smiling? It's because the backbone of their business is the smile. Disney is synonymous with the smile. Everything from a funny little mouse to a spellbound princess depends on producing the same end result—a smiling customer!

Smile Science—Who Knew?

Scientists at the University of North Carolina at Charlotte found that the smile is perceived by customers as an indicator of competence, positive mood and the desire to provide quality service. Employees' smiles can also have big payoffs, even when the smiles are intentional. In studies concerning the service industry, researchers found that customers consistently felt they received quality service from employees that delivered service with a smile. It did not matter to the customers whether the smile was perceived as genuine or fake. (Pugh 2001)

Smiling and Social Networking

Mary met her match online. After years of waiting for the right guy to cross her path, she decided to join an online dating service. While reviewing the profiles of available men, she felt an instant connection with Todd because of his great smile. Mary's hunch was right. Todd and Mary really hit it off. They are getting ready to celebrate their four year wedding anniversary with friends and family. Social media has changed the way the world communicates. Over 15% of people have met their current partner online.

Worldwide, more than a billion people now use social networking sites like Facebook and Myspace. Are you one of the billion that has posted some photos of yourself online? People put a lot of value in those pictures—more than you may realize. Whether you like it or not, people are forming opinions of you by viewing those pictures. And consider, those photos can live on in cyberspace forever.

Smile Magic—What's Happening?

It turns out that observers are astoundingly accurate in judging some personality traits from online photos. If you're exhibiting a genuine smile in the photos, most people will perceive you as an extrovert with positive self-esteem and good health.

Surprisingly, most of these observations would be right. But here's the catch—it's got to be an authentic smile. Otherwise the smile will come across as insincere and phony. In other words, you can't outrun your personality online.

In addition, researchers discovered that social networks really do have clusters of happiness. Those smiles being shared, whether online or in person, are contagious and can spread by three degrees of separation. So, a friend of a friend of a friend can eventually catch the positive feelings from the smile.

Smile: Happiness Is Right Under Your Nose!

People who are surrounded by happy people are more likely to become happy themselves because of feelings that spread within social networks.

———————— ————————

Smile Science—Who Knew?

Scientists at the University of Texas at Austin found that observers were able to accurately judge individuals' personality traits in ten areas, such as extraversion, agreeableness, openness, likeability, etc., based solely on their posture and facial expressions, such as their smile, seen in their photos. (Naumann, et al. 2009)

Smiling and Judgment

"Your smile must come from within and your eyes must light up." Thousands of teenage girls listened intently to these instructions during their audition. Their hope was to become one of the very special girls selected to present medals at the 2008 Olympics in Beijing, China.

The Chinese government spent an unprecedented $44 billion on the 2008 games. This was more money than the cost of the five preceding Olympic Games put together. Between media coverage and tourism, China knew that the world would be watching and in the process judging them. Getting the rest of the world to perceive China in the way the Chinese government wanted, was highly important to the Chinese authorities. For some of the Chinese people, their job was all about demonstrating the right type of smile. Sometimes it was even carried to the extreme, when shopkeepers were threatened with arrest if they did not smile to customers during the games.

Recognizing that the smile is a universal symbol of happiness doesn't mean it comes easy to all cultures. Typically, children in China are taught to suppress emotion, not to exhibit it. At the auditions to be a medal presenter, one young girl shared, "The most important thing I can do is to smile to show the world that ours is a land of etiquette." She described that learning to show her smile was challenging and demonstrated a technique they were being taught. Holding a chopstick across her mouth, she expressed, "We have to show between six and eight teeth, and we must be able to hold a chopstick horizontal like this."

Smile Magic—What's Happening?

Perhaps you may think that the Chinese government went to extreme measures to encourage their citizens to share smiles during the 2008 Olympic Games. However, considering that people judge individuals more trustworthy and approachable when they exhibit genuine smiles, they believed it was worth the effort.

The smile is seen as a sign of cooperation. Whether we like it or not, people are constantly judging us by our appearance. It happens in a fraction of a second. Possessing a genuine smile and sharing it ranks high as a way to be perceived as a kind individual with a willingness to connect.

China isn't the only culture that has invested in smile training to counter long held societal norms of not expressing emotions. Recognizing the power of the smile in international business negotiations, smile therapy sessions are being offered in Japan. On a lunch break, professionals can get hooked up to a smile machine. The 30 minute sessions are designed to lift the participant's mouth muscles and spirits as well as company profits—all because of their found smile.

Smile Science—Who Knew?

Scientists in England discovered that an individual's genuine smile is associated with personal positive attributes. When participants were asked to evaluate identical faces, some smiling and some not, the smiling faces were judged to be more intelligent, kind, social and attractive. (O'Doherty, et al. 2003)

Smiling and Advertising

Smile! You're the star of Super Ad Sunday. At a cost of $100,000 a second or $3 million for a 30 second slot, big bucks are being spent to get you to smile on Super Bowl Sunday. A Nielson study of 25,000 households recently revealed that 51% of people viewing the Super Bowl prefer watching the commercials more than the action on the field.

People like and remember ads that tickle their funny bone. That's why business advice in advertisements can come from a talking lizard or pig rather than a bean counter. Advertisers are savvy. They know that having the most popular ad will result in millions of dollars in free publicity. Favorite commercials are ranked and replayed on all types of social media—free of charge.

Smile Magic—What's Happening?

When an ad can make you smile, we identify that positive feeling with the product. The most successful ads have been those that follow this strategy and get you to smile. In fact, researchers actually found that the more a commercial describes the product, the less successful the ad will probably be in consumer appeal. When it comes to successful ads, it turns out that *more is definitely less.*

Businesses frequently engage in tactics to have us put our money where our smiles are. "Smile Tagging" is one of these latest marketing strategies. The Kraft Company has cleverly introduced its own version of the "like" button on Facebook. After installing the application, you can use a Kraft browser plug-in to bookmark something that makes you smile. Using your computer's webcam you can then take a picture of yourself. That smiling picture is then sent to the smile tagging Facebook page. Anyone choosing to click on your smile will then be taken directly to the page that made you smile in the first place.

Smile: Happiness Is Right Under Your Nose!

Smile Tagging is a clever and fun branding strategy that gets us to smile. My personal favorite is the talking lizard. If the image of that little green guy conjured up a smile, then tag, you're it!

———————— ————————

Smile Science—Who Knew?

After studying hundreds of Super Bowl ads that aired over the last decade, scientists found that the most successful ads were the ones that didn't talk much about the product. Instead, humorous and creative ads that brought a smile to the viewer were the most popular. (Tomkovick, et al. 2010)

Smiling and Renewable Resources

People from all over the world have done it. Thousands have gathered in places like Croatia, France, Germany and America to do it. People from these and other countries have come together to break the Guinness world record to create the largest human smiley face. Recently on a sunny afternoon at Whitchurch-Stouffville near Toronto, Canada, once again history was made when more than 3,000 people smiled their way to the new record. Smiles generate smiles—they're a renewable resource!

Currently, more than 140 countries are involved in an international smile campaign. Globally, they are all part of the Art of Living Foundation. This foundation is one of the largest non-governmental, volunteer based, humanitarian and educational organizations. The nonprofit group seeks to spread happiness across continents through meeting with people and sending a message of creating personal peace and less stress in our lives.

In 2009 they organized "smile campaigns" in several U.S. cities. Volunteers with cameras spread out looking for anyone willing to stop and have their smile photographed. The pictures were subsequently uploaded to the organization's website. Since then, this foundation has transcended borders and spread millions of smiles around the world.

Smile Magic—What's Happening?

Regardless of culture, people can spontaneously display smiles to one another as a simple act of kindness and peace. Smiling is positively contagious, involves no politics, no religion and no money.

The *gifted smile* is a renewable resource. It is positive energy that spontaneously regenerates itself. Free of charge.

Smile Science—Who Knew?

Smiles are a powerful renewable resource. Social scientist, Barbara Fredrickson from the University of Michigan, has shared, "Genuine smiles reflect perhaps the most crucial renewable human resource of our times—positive emotions. As they accumulate and compound, genuine smiles and heartfelt positive emotions transform people and communities for the better. You can hardly prevent yourself from being moved and transformed by the beauty, joy and hope created by the simple act of smiling." (Fredrickson 2009)

Smiling and Culture

Singapore is one of the safest, richest and cleanest countries in the world. A global study also found Singapore to be the happiest country in Asia. Singaporeans are a happy people and now they are being encouraged to spread this emotion throughout their country, by sharing their smile with others.

As part of a smile campaign, mirrors have been placed throughout Singapore at selected bus stops with a tagline which includes, "Champion a smile". The purpose is to have Singaporeans take a moment to view themselves smiling in the mirrors, and then reflect this smile to others. The campaign's hope is that the gracious gesture of the smile will spread and continue to be passed along throughout the country. The project is part of a kindness movement in Singapore.

This isn't the first smile campaign that Singapore has undertaken. In 2006, the government sponsored the "four million smiles" project to help welcome business travelers and tourists to the country. Smiling Singaporeans are certainly sending the right message to visitors. The country is judged as being one of the most welcoming and successful in the world.

Smile Magic—What's Happening?

Singapore is not the only country that has taken steps to initiate smile campaigns. Because people judge individuals who demonstrate sincere smiles as being cooperative and friendly, other countries have also undertaken steps to encourage their inhabitants to smile. Russia is a culture that has had a preference toward expressing neutral faces in public. Wanting to foster a friendlier atmosphere for visitors, the government put up posters in Moscow's subway stations urging the public to smile. The signs show a smiling, cheerful Russian metro worker expressing the words, "It's an inexpensive way to improve your looks."

France has also tried its hand at smile campaigns. As part of a hospitality program, booklets of "smile checks" were distributed to tourists. When they received particularly good service, visitors could fill out the smile checks with the employee's name and mail it to the French Tourist Office. The hope was that the French workers would be motivated to smile more, while providing friendly service to tourists and also having the chance to win prizes for their smiles.

Despite the best of efforts, it is not always easy to get a culture to express their smiles, if it is not their norm. Then there is always the possibility that the smile's message will get lost in translation. People exchange smiles for different reasons.

Recently, I had the chance to live in France for some months. As the weather changed, I needed a warmer jacket. I went to a little shop and tried on a coat and asked the clerk if it was waterproof. We were both having trouble understanding each other, when suddenly the salesperson picked up a water bottle and sprayed water on the jacket I was trying on. We both realized it was waterproof when the liquid slid down the coat. I was smiling from surprise and shock from the sudden shower, while the clerk was smiling because she had accomplished her job—trying to answer my question. We were both smiling, but for very different reasons. In the future, when I would pass the boutique wearing my waterproof jacket, we both smiled, but with different accents!

Smile Science—Who Knew?

People have deeply rooted cultural differences in how and why they smile. In scientific studies, Americans and Australians were able to correctly identify which country participants were from by simply viewing photographs of smiling individuals. Neutral faces in the photos provided no clue to the person's culture, but when participants viewed smiling photographs, they were better able to guess the individual's country. (Marsh, et al. 2007)

Smiling and Contagion

Jell-O Pudding is out to make everyone in the United States smile. High above the streets of New York City sits an electronic billboard which the people of America control. The billboard is a huge rendering of Jell-O's Pudding Face Mood Meter. The billboard calculates the mood of America by monitoring, in real time, the number of happy ☺ or sad ☹ emoticons people are tweeting.

The face on the billboard changes expression to reflect the fluctuation in both smile and frown percentages. Here's the best part. As the mood of the nation begins to dip, based on the emoticons, Jell-O quickly deploys free pudding coupons to frowners via Twitter, so they'll catch a happier mood. Before you know it, the billboard is sporting a larger than life smiling pudding face again.

Smile Magic—What's Happening?

Smiles really are contagious. As social beings, we simply can't help ourselves. Our brains are hardwired to mirror the expressions and moods of others. The effects of emotional contagion are so strong that some scientists believe we understand others first—not by thinking—but by our feelings.

Even infants, only a few weeks after birth, can mimic an unfamiliar expression like the smile on a stranger's face. This capability fine tunes our capacity to empathize, which may have significantly contributed to the survival of the human species over thousands of years.

The human phenomenon of emotional contagion is so powerful that when subliminal smiles are flashed for a fraction of a second in front of unsuspecting individuals they feel happier without knowing why. A study, conducted over a span of 20 years, also showed that the mood picked up by the smile is not only contagious but its ability to spread is profound. The positive effects of a single smile can travel to your friends' friends' friends, or up to three degrees of separation away.

Neuroscientists are beginning to realize that our brain's system of mirror neurons allows us to simulate what another person is feeling by simply observing him. A leading scientist in this field, Marco Iacoboni, states, "When I see you smiling, my mirror neurons for smiling fire up, too, initiating a cascade of neural activity that evokes the feeling we typically associate with a smile. I don't need to make any inferences on what you are feeling: I experience immediately and effortlessly (in a milder form, of course) what you are experiencing."

Smile Science—Who Knew?

Smiles really are contagious. Scientists at Uppsala University in Sweden found that when participants were mimicking a person's facial expression, such as the smile, it caused physical responses in the participant's body that were identical to those in the smile's originator. The receiver's body reacted physically as if he were the initiator of the smile. (Dimburg, et al. 2000)

Smiling and Loneliness

Feeling alone has nothing to do with the number of friends you have. I know people who have hundreds of friends, and still feel lonely. Conversely, there are some people that live in solitude and never feel lonely.

Loneliness is only a problem when it comes with a gnawing sense of emptiness from a lack of social connectedness. Any kind of transition in life can increase our loneliness factor. When I turned 40, I decided to reinvent myself. I changed my profession and moved across the country. During that time, I experienced loneliness.

Not knowing anyone in my new home, I felt socially disconnected. One morning, I decided to take a risk and step out of my loneliness rut. Armed with a bag of change, I made my way to the local newspaper box. As each person stepped up to the box, I used my change to buy a paper and present it to the stranger with a smile. Talk about getting a bang for my buck! I will never forget the beautiful smiles of surprise and gratitude I received from strangers. The smiles instantly lifted my spirit, spiraled into interesting conversations, and connected me to something greater than my sense of loneliness.

I gained confidence from those shared paper box smiles which instantly connected me to others. The experience motivated me to try something else outside my comfort zone—ballroom dancing. Growing up sick, I never had the chance to participate in physical activities. I had always wanted to learn to dance, and now was my chance. Smiling, as a cover up for my anxiety, I marched myself into a dance studio. At first, I felt like a turtle hiding in its shell on the dance floor, but soon I was joyfully smiling as I twisted and turned. It felt fantastic. I was quickly hooked, and my loneliness was a thing of the past. My smile helped to boost my confidence to try something different, which led to finding a new family of dance friends.

Smile Magic—What's Happening?

Sometimes having the courage to share a smile with a stranger can change a life. Not just yours, but also the person receiving the smile. A dear friend who is a philanthropist shared, "If we have nothing else—at least give a smile." We never know how much a person may be silently hurting. A recent global survey revealed that the number one fear in the world is the thought of being alone.

Trust that your genuine smile can desensitize you from fears of imperfection or rejection, which may be holding you back from connecting with others. Your smile will help open doors and attract positive relationships. Smiles that are shared sincerely are baby steps that can be taken to help obliterate loneliness.

———————— ————————

Smile Science—Who Knew?

Scientists found that people associate a smiling face with someone they already know, even if the person is a complete stranger. Your smile helps you connect with others and can put you in a positive and familiar light with them. (Lander and Metcalfe 2007)

Smiling and Competence

If you close your eyes, smile and click your heels three times, maybe you'll wind up in Hollywood. Young people want to be rich and famous, and they want it in an instant. In a national study of 18 to 25 year olds, 81% stated their top goal in life is to be rich and 51% want to be famous.

Reality shows, like "American Idol", plant the idea that stardom is but a phone call away. After auditioning thousands and shattering many delusional dreamers, a handful of hopefuls make it onto the show. Once there, cracking the winning code takes more than just talent.

Celebrity judges encourage the contestants to smile. Jennifer Lopez, who has been one of the judges, has even stated during her critique of a contestant, "I love somebody who smiles while they are singing, it lights up the stage." The smiling contestant eventually went on to become one of the season's finalists.

Smile Magic—What's Happening?

The contestants on this and other reality shows are encouraged to smile because it helps them to connect with the audience. Some of the participants actually go through *smile makeovers*. Not only is the smile found to be attractive, it helps the contestants appear more accessible, genuine and competent. With so many talented young people stretching beyond their limits to obtain fame and fortune, sometimes having an incredible voice is not enough to win a contest like "American Idol."

Having a beautiful smile can give a rising star an edge that puts their performance ahead of the competition. The smile is part of the *x or it factor*. It is part of a total package that has been shown to produce smiling winners.

——————— ———————

Smile Science—Who Knew?

Scientists at Western Carolina University found that your smile sends a message to others that you are accessible, intelligent and competent. Researchers found that people judge a smiling facial expression with positive attributes such as sociability, sincerity and competence. (Abel and Watters 2005)

Smiling and Thought Control

Evan over-analyzes everything. Sometimes he feels like his thoughts are out to get him. Thinking for him is exhausting. His mind seems to run 24/7. Evan is even thinking in his sleep—trying constantly to come up with solutions—sometimes about his inability to stop thinking. It's a vicious cycle.

Evan wishes that there were some natural way to just shut his brain off for at least a little bit, from time to time. He has tried meditation, hypnosis and biofeedback. Nothing has worked because he just can't seem to stop thinking while doing the exercises.

Evan is not alone. It is estimated that the average person has around 50,000 thoughts a day. Most of us have at least one negative thought about ourselves every 26 minutes. Thinking can often feel like it is out of our control.

Smile Magic—What's Happening?

We like to think that there is a logical cause and effect to our thinking process. The truth is that thoughts are fleeting. Sometimes, there is no rhyme or reason to our thoughts. They can change from positive to negative in an instant and vice versa.

The problem with negative thoughts is the sense that we have no control over them. We have two options to deal with negative thoughts. First, one can choose to analyze them to death. If you give a thought great importance and ponder it over and over, it can snowball and spiral into nonproductive behavior, sadness or even depression.

On the other hand, instead of intensely thinking about a negative thought, it is more productive to take a positive action to combat it. Forcing yourself to smile is an active step you can take that can bring you to a more peaceful state of mind and into the moment. For example, if I ask you not to think of pink elephants it is almost impossible not to think of them. Taking concrete action is more effective than telling yourself not to think negative thoughts.

Smiling and Thought Control

Research has shown that if we want to cancel a negative thought, we can take action such as remembering three positive things in our life that will make us smile. The three things can be very simple. For example, picture yourself taking a walk in nature, reading a good book or savoring something delicious—whatever makes you smile. It's not a complicated process, but it allows you to take action to change thinking patterns. The premise is that you increase your daily diet of smiles in order to cancel negative thinking. The suggested prescription is "three smiles to each grimace", to help you take control and produce happier thoughts.

Smile Science—Who Knew?

Smiling can help us control negative thinking patterns. Scientists discovered a 3 to 1 ratio for happier thinking. In other words, to take control of our thinking process, it has been shown that we need at least three positive thoughts that bring a smile to lift us up for every negative thought that drags us down. The lead scientist of the research shared, "We need three or more smiles to each grimace." (Fredrickson 2009)

Smiling and Relationships

Would you want to be around another you? When asked about his marriage, Michael describes it as being filled with complaints, whining and emotional tantrums. He is exasperated, and takes a big sigh before he even begins to describe his partner's behavior! Relationships are hard work. Even the most caring of couples can have difficulty holding things together over the long run.

Have you ever been in a disagreement with your partner? When we feel the need to be understood—we fine tune our emotional antennae to a high frequency. This is especially true if someone is important to us and we respect their opinion. During these times, the subtlest of facial gestures can be construed as either messages of acceptance or rejection. Has anyone ever rolled their eyes at you during an argument? How did it make you feel? Were you hurt or disgusted? If so, you're not alone.

Smile Magic—What's Happening?

Research shows that our nonverbal expressions send powerful communication messages about our interpersonal relationships. The rolling of the eyes can be a recipe for disaster. It is one of the worst nonverbal gestures. The genuine smile, however, ranks high as one of the best shared expressions. The sincere smile is perceived as a sign of understanding and acceptance. Our smiles deliver positive emotional messages of connection to people that we care about.

Researchers can actually predict the lasting power of a marriage by studying the rate of nonverbal positive and negative interactions between couples. When asked to describe good and not so good relationship situations, those couples that display the most sincere emotional signs, like the smile, during the discourse are inevitably the most happily married. By quantifying the observations a ratio has emerged, which is five positive interactions to each negative one. Applying this formula, researchers have been able to predict with 94% accuracy, which couples will later divorce.

Smiling and Relationships

Couples in lasting relationships positively influence each other's moods. They do this routinely, unconsciously and multiple times through their nonverbal behavior. Such is the case with Herbert and Zelma, who hold the record for one of the longest marriages on the books. Together for 86 years, when interviewed about the lasting power of their marriage, they gazed at each other while sharing a loving smile.

Even before hitting the altar, having a natural tendency to smile can be an indicator for a positive relationship. When researchers examined childhood photos of 65 year olds, the big toothy smilers in the earlier photos turned out to have happier and longer lasting marriages. Those who frowned in the earlier photos, before they were ever married, were five times more likely to be divorced later in life. So before you slip that ring on that finger, you may want to first check out your partner's smile in the family photo albums before saying, "I do!"

Smile Science—Who Knew?

Scientists at DePauw University examined childhood and college yearbook pictures of people over the age of 65. After scoring the smile strength of the photos, only 11% of the biggest smilers had been divorced while 31% of the frowners had experienced a broken marriage. People who frowned in their youthful photos were 5 times more likely to get a divorce, than those who had smiled. (Hertenstein, et al. 2009)

Smiling and Self-Esteem

What do you think your life would be like, if you couldn't smile? Born with a facial deformity, Pinki is a little girl who was unable to experience the joy that comes from smiling freely. Because of her severe cleft lip, she was ostracized by her community in rural India. Tortured and tormented because of her deformity, Pinki wasn't even allowed to attend school. Many in her community believed she was cursed by God.

Pinki's cleft lip seriously compromised her self-esteem. Some villagers would even demonstrate their revulsion and fear by throwing rocks at her. Social acceptance has a direct impact on our self-esteem. The inability to smile because of a facial deformity can be devastating to a person's self-image. Such was the case with Pinki who became an introverted social outcast.

Then one day, Pinki's life was totally turned around. Pinki received a gift. Volunteers from the charity, Smile Train, performed a life transforming operation. That precious gift gave Pinki the uninhibited ability to freely share her beautiful smile. In 2009, the little girl's heartwarming story became a movie entitled, *Smile Pinki*. This work about Pinki's life went on to win an academy award for the best short documentary. She even had the opportunity to attend the internationally televised Academy Awards Ceremony held in Hollywood, California. Pinki went from being a social outcast to becoming a local celebrity with a smile seen by thousands.

Smile Magic—What's Happening?

Have you ever been told you have a beautiful smile? If so, such a compliment affects both your well-being and self-confidence. Not having the ability to freely smile can be physically and psychologically damaging. Dr. Nigel Carter, Chief Executive of the British Dental Health Foundation, shared that not having a healthy smile, "...can affect self-confidence, image and even how we are perceived by other people."

Smiling and Self-Esteem

Sometimes our acceptance by others is judged by our appearance. Our smile is so powerful that some people, who are physically unable to smile due to a health condition, learn to express this emotion in other ways. For example, some learn to *smile through their eyes*. Most of us judge a person to be more attractive and intelligent when they are smiling, than when they aren't.

An interesting study tracked 110 coeds over the course of 30 years. After reviewing how the women were fairing over time at ages 21, 27, 43 and 52, the researchers found that women who had expressed the most genuine smiles in their college yearbooks had greater life satisfaction and self-esteem later in life. In addition, the study concluded that the biggest, most sincere smilers became "...more organized, mentally focused and achievement oriented and less susceptible to repeated and prolonged experiences of negative effect." This study supports the profound connection that being able to genuinely sport a sincere smile enhances lifelong personal self-esteem.

Smile Science—Who Knew?

Scientists in the Netherlands found that when we cannot smile, it can lead others to misinterpret our mood, intelligence or intentions. Researchers also found that participants who were greeted with a smiling face had significantly lower anxiety about themselves. As a result, the participant's self-esteem also improved. (Martijn, et al. 2010)

Smiling and Education

The "Art of Smiling" has been the subject of the largest class in the history of Harvard University. Just a few short years ago, the class started as an experiment in the Psychology Department with only 6 students. Now up to 20% of Harvard's undergraduate population has applied to enroll in the class in a single semester. Thousands have taken the "Art of Smiling" seriously at Harvard, contributing to its enormous success and popularity.

The course's curriculum looks at contemporary research with the purpose of learning the "Science of Happiness." Universally, psychology is going through a happiness revolution. Psychology traditionally has focused on what is wrong or missing in a person's life. Positive psychology is different. It focuses on what's right in your life. *Smile Courses* like Harvard's have spread to educational institutions and organizations throughout the world.

Smile Magic—What's Happening?

Many people believe we live in troubled times. In addition, technology has changed the way people communicate on this planet. Now with the advent of social media, news can travel and spread at lightning fast rates. The news of an economic crisis or act of terrorism can quickly spread online causing widespread panic, and even revolution. The world is ready for some happiness and the positive psychology movement has been embraced and is doing its share to spread a different message.

Positive psychology plants seeds of hope that we can control how we respond to events in our lives. This response affects our level of happiness. Recently, even the U.S. military has mandated, for the first time, army-wide training in positive psychology.

A big emphasis of this psychology is to develop *emotional resilience*. More than a million soldiers will be taught basic concepts based upon the work of Martin Seligman, who is considered the founder of positive psychology. The primary thrust of his work is to focus on what is going right in your life, to express gratitude and to analyze and correct negative views of ambiguous events. Dr. Seligman writes that when resilience is practiced, "It is possible to be happier, to feel more satisfied, to be more engaged with life, find more meaning, have higher hopes and probably even laugh and smile more, regardless of one's circumstances."

The principles of *emotional resilience* may seem surprisingly simple, but they work. Research shows that happiness is not necessarily found in extrinsic factors like money or work. If you earn $5 million, you won't necessarily be any happier than someone earning $50 thousand, as long as your basic needs are secure. It's the little everyday things that bring the most happiness—not an abundance of wealth or possessions. It's the things that make us grateful and bring a smile that have the biggest payoff. That's why a primary exercise in positive psychology is to keep a gratitude journal. Students are instructed to write regularly, expressing gratitude for simple things that bring them happiness—the simple things in life that make them smile.

Smile Science—Who Knew?

Social scientists are teaching the education of happiness throughout the world. Curriculums that examine what makes people happy focus on gratitude. Unfortunately, many people take the good things in their life for granted. Research shows that taking time to express gratitude can bring real happiness. "This includes savoring the little things in life, from people to food, from nature to a smile." (Ben-Shahar and Achor 2006)

Smiling and Creativity

Smiling outside the box, Bren Bataclan, has become a bit of an escape artist. After losing his job as a computer graphics teacher, he started painting quirky cartoon characters. Fearing he may become just another starving artist, Bren came up with a crazy idea. He decided to actually give his paintings away, asking only one thing in return. He attached this note to each canvas: "This painting is yours if you promise to smile at random people more often."

Bren solicited the help of his friends when they would travel. He asked them to place his art in simple places like public park benches. These efforts have made Bren's free art smile project an international success. His giveaway art has landed him smiles throughout the U.S. and in more than 20 countries. It also resulted in multiple commissions for his murals and paintings.

Smile Magic—What's Happening?

What inspires you to create? Surprisingly, studies show that activities that make you smile can help spark your imagination. One reason is because creative genius, connections and *aha* moments are more likely to occur when you are in a relaxed state. The act of smiling brings balance and calmness to oneself. Smiling helps get your creative juices flowing.

What goes on in your brain when you create? You quiet your front left cortex and fire up the right side. That's why activities that are fun or cause you to smile fuel the process. They help get you to the right side of your brain. Breaking usual thinking patterns—especially stressful ones—assist you to zone out and get into a creative flow.

After teaching creativity seminars for years, I learned that most people secretly wish they could be more creative. Unfortunately, many have an assumption that they don't have artistic talent or ability. This is incorrect. We are all born with tremendous creative capability. However, we live in a left brain dominant society. This can play havoc with our creative intelligence. Our creativity

Smiling and Creativity

can get rusty, blocked or downgraded in the thinking process.

Here's the good news. Creativity is a skill. This means you can sharpen or reawaken your creative talent. Creativity enhances all aspects of life. You don't have to be an aspiring artist to reap the benefits of the process. Everything, including life transitions, is better handled with innovative thinking. So consider getting into the right side/state of your mind. Smile, and fire up your creative electrical impulses.

Smile Science—Who Knew?

Scientists at the University of Western Ontario found that smiling can enhance creative problem solving. When participants viewed happy videos of smiling and laughing babies, they were better able to solve problems—thinking more creatively and innovatively than those participants who watched sad videos. (Nadler, et al. 2010)

Smiling and Income

Actress, Julia Roberts, really does have a million dollar smile. Plastic surgeons share that Julia has led the pack as the most requested celebrity smile from patients. Recently, the actress was paid a whopping $1.6 million by an Italian coffee company, just to look into the camera and smile.

In the ad, Julia is posing for a famous artist, Botticelli, who is painting her portrait. The artist wants her to smile, which she won't do until she gets a sip of the Italian brew. In a clip that lasts only 45 seconds, Julia doesn't even speak. Words are not necessary because it's Julia's beautiful smile that does all the talking.

Smile Magic—What's Happening?

Do you think your smile is worth a million dollars? Your smile may be worth more than you realize. People who smile regularly have been shown to make more money, have greater income, be more productive and have more job opportunities. Sincere smiles are a type of social currency that is valued by society.

Perhaps you have been part of a big business deal that involved lots of statistical analysis, hours of investigation and countless meetings. Many times there is an additional factor that can play a major role in the final decision—going with your instinct or gut feelings!

What are the primary influencers of gut feelings? Typically, nonverbal behavior can influence as much as 75% of our judgment. People's expressions, like the sincerity of a person's smile, can be seen as a sign of cooperation and trust that can weigh heavily on such important decisions. Social scientists have found that, "When people don't return smiles, this can lead to breakdowns in the conversation. Smiles encourage collaboration and productivity in work—if more genuine smiles are seen in a

Smiling and Income

meeting, that meeting is likely to achieve its aims more quickly and with fewer difficulties."

Our smiles have cash value. They are a type of social currency that society is willing to pay more to see. Have you ever given a waitress, who served you with an engaging smile, an extra tip? If so, you have been a part of the smile economy.

Smile Science—Who Knew?

The smile is a type of social currency. Scientists in England were able to calculate what people were willing to pay to receive genuine versus polite smiles. They found that genuine smiles had a higher payout. People consistently chose to play against opponents with genuine smiles rather than fake smiles, even when that meant they were less likely to win and they realized it. A genuine smile adds value to a person and their conversation, thereby influencing how we view them and how we evaluate monetary decisions related to them. (Shore and Heerey 2011)

Smiling and Technology

What can be better than a humanoid robot that can smile? How about a humanoid robot that knows, intuitively, when to smile? Scientists are figuring out how to get more intelligence into the world of artificial intelligence. Inspired by how babies learn to communicate, scientists are creating robots that know when to smile to convey proper emotions.

Technology is poised for a breakthrough that will lead to a new generation of intelligent machines. It is predicted that 80% of active internet users and Fortune 500 companies will have an avatar or a presence in a virtual community in the next few years. Scientists have been working for decades to create technology that will allow interaction between humans and computers to be more intuitive and natural. Can you imagine a baby robot that can look into your eyes, smile, and also learn like a human infant?

Smile Magic—What's Happening?

Expressions, like the smile, help robots appear more human. Scientists have found that when robots, that have been programmed to display what is perceived to be a genuine smile, approach humans, we are less likely to be fearful. Women in particular have allowed virtual beings to come closer if they approach with a genuine smile rather than none at all. Even mechanical smiles are judged in the same manner as human smiles. The virtual smile is seen as a friendly gesture that sends a message of trust and connection.

Although it may seem like something out of a science fiction movie, it is projected that in the near future, robots will be commonplace as personal assistants and household maids. The personal robotic industry is booming with a growth rate of 400% a year. Add in the dramatic drop in manufacturing costs, and an international technological explosion is close at hand.

In some parts of the world, such as Japan, "Service robots are currently being used in all walks of life, from child-minding robots to those that care for the elderly." The technology is so sophisticated, that it can be controlled remotely by a mobile phone or a personal computer. In other information fields, there is smile recognition technology in place that allows a user to place an order over the internet by simply smiling and nodding. You can even donate your smile over your webcam to help researchers at the Massachusetts Institute of Technology who are involved in groundbreaking work for those with autism and communication challenges.

Is it too creepy to think of replacing your doggy with a smiling robot as your best friend? Well, ready or not—the smiling androids are coming!

Smile Science—Who Knew?

Scientists at McGill University in Canada found that by just clicking on a smile, even one that is virtual (one on our computers), users had a rise in self-esteem from seeing the virtual smile. This has led researchers to decipher and analyze virtual smiles as an effective tool for teaching and learning. (Baacus, et al. 2004)

Smiling and Attitude

Spence is having his big 40th birthday next week. He's got a great job, a beautiful family and is well respected in his community. There is only one problem—he's miserable. The truth is Spence feels like he needs a vacation from himself. He knows he should be happy and wishes he could just have an attitude adjustment.

Spence is not alone in his frustration. After studying 2 million people in more than 70 countries for the last 4 decades, it was concluded that, "Miserable middle age is a global phenomenon." No matter where you live in the world, whether you're rich or poor, married or single, sooner or later mental distress will probably rear its ugly head and mess with yours.

Smile Magic—What's Happening?

Most of us assume that mental distress or having a bad attitude gets worse as we get older, but this is incorrect. Actually, most of us bottom out in our 40's. We then begin to bounce back in our 50's and 60's. After studying the trajectory of a typical person's mood or attitude throughout life, researchers concluded that by 70, if you are still physically fit, you will be as happy and mentally healthy as a 20 year old.

What matters most in determining if we have a good attitude in life? It turns out that 50% of our happiness factor is genetic and only 10% is dependent on external factors like income. A whopping 40% of our happiness is based on our intentional behavior. In other words, much of our happiness is within our conscious control. Researchers have found that our positive emotions—the simple things that make us smile—are the hallmark of happiness and can lead to upward spirals in mood and behavior.

Seeing happiness as a skill presents tremendous benefits. This means by practicing positive actions that make us smile,

Smiling and Attitude

we can successfully change our emotions and bring about happier lives. This is true even when we cannot change our genetic predisposition or external factors. Simple things that bring a smile—such as practicing acts of kindness, taking a soothing bath or listening to your favorite music can make a big difference. It's a cumulative process that leads to a positive attitude. Together they add up to the 40% of the pie that is in our control for a happy life.

Smile Science—Who Knew?

Scientists in Great Britain studied more than 26,000 online participants to determine what helps to lift a person's attitude and create a happier mood. The conclusion, that thinking about one positive thing that had happened the day before that made you smile, was the most effective mood enhancer. This quick and simple technique provided a 15% boost in happiness. (Wiseman 2009)

Smiling and Leadership

Do you carry a smile in your pocket? Known by many as the *smiling president*, Franklin D. Roosevelt's face of hope is indelibly stamped on more than 18 billion dimes in America. During a time of massive unemployment and global economic stagnation, Roosevelt, became the president of the Great Depression. Even Senator Hiram Johnson from California, conceded, "We have exchanged for a frown in the White House a smile."

No one understood the impact of the smile better than Roosevelt. In contrast to the harsh times, Roosevelt realized that his uplifting smile was being perceived as a message of hope and comfort to much of the world. Interestingly, although he gave the impression of being a natural and gifted orator, Roosevelt suffered from stage fright.

Before a speech, Roosevelt would practice not only his words, but also his smile, so that they would flow spontaneously and effortlessly. Even when his audience was not able to see him, such as in the case of his radio fireside chats, Roosevelt would still begin with a gesture and a smile before speaking into the microphone. He realized that the listeners would be searching for a ray of hope, for something they could not see but could sense: his smile.

Smile Magic—What's Happening?

Here's a news flash—being tight-lipped and straight faced does not make for the most effective leaders. Followers look to leaders as influencers. What does this mean? People naturally look to the person at the top or in control for emotional guidance. Study after study shows that if a leader is upbeat and can express it in positive cues—such as in their genuine smile—this will positively influence and motivate followers. This is true even during times of crisis, pressure or extreme challenge. Conversely, showing dismay, disapproval or fear in a leader's outward behavior is inevitably non-productive.

Smiling and Leadership

Americans interpreted FDR's smile as a sign of hope during troubled times. People are always highly scrutinizing their leader's behavior and emotional cues. This is what people are naturally inclined to do. It is why a leader's mood is of the utmost importance to their followers. Whether outwardly good or bad, it is emotionally contagious. Followers inevitably *catch* their leader's mood, and act on it accordingly. Many times this happens without the followers even being aware of how their mindset has been influenced.

This phenomenon of emotional contagion is extremely important to leadership. It drives the focus, behavior and direction for change in an organization. "Moods that start at the top, tend to move the fastest, because everyone watches the boss." Nonverbal expressions, like the smile, are extreme influencers. For example, if you put two people in a room facing each other without any verbal communication, their moods will converge. Here's the most important result of these studies: eventually the less expressive individual will take on the mood of the more facially expressive—such as the smiling individual.

Gallup scientists studied more than 1 million work teams,

and interviewed more than 10,000 followers across the world to determine why people choose to follow certain individuals as leaders. The key characteristics of trust, compassion, stability and hope were the primary themes that emerged from the study. A leader's genuine smile is an asset that demonstrates these attributes and acknowledges these needs in their followers. This is because people judge leaders that exhibit authentic smiles as being more trustworthy, compassionate and intelligent.

——————— ———————

Smile Science—Who Knew?

A leader's mood can influence large scale systems and is emotionally contagious. Scientists from the University of Minnesota and Michigan State University found that followers are influenced by a leader's positive emotional expressions, such as the smile. Also, participants viewed leaders that were able to express emotional cues, such as the smile, as being more effective in their leadership style. (Bono and Ilies 2006)

Smiling and Listening

Each year more than 100 goats are deployed on a mission in downtown Los Angeles. Their official assignment is to munch their way through unruly invasive weeds in a city park on Bunker Hill. As an alternative to pesticides and mowing, the goats work for food on goat time. The weeds get chomped when the goats are hungry. As a result they stick around for awhile and usually draw lots of attention.

Thousands of passengers on the Metro are entertained as they pass the scene on their daily commute to work. National Public Radio has aired a story about the goats. Listening to the story you can't see the reporter or the interviewees, but you can hear their smiles as they describe the "weed-whacking goats."

See if you aren't moved to smile as you listen to some of the comments that were shared by interviewees, "There are baby goats and mama goats, but they are all hungry goats";

"They make everybody smile and laugh"; "It creates this kind of warmth, this unity"; and "I think it's hysterical." Mission accomplished for the goats. Not only do they clear the land, but they leave it fertilized with a trail of smiles!

Smile Magic—What's Happening?

If you were listening to this story on the radio, do you think it would conjure up a smile or two for you? Would you be able to hear the smiles of the reporters as they described the goats mowing through the landscape?

Smiles can be heard—even when they can't be seen. Listeners can positively identify if a speaker is smiling—even when they cannot see the individual. People speak at 100 to 175 words per minute, but they can listen intelligently at 600 to 700 words per minute. This means that much of what we comprehend from a person's communication is greatly affected by facial expressions, voice inflections and tonality—elements beyond the spoken words. This phenomenon is so powerful that telemarketers have been shown to have higher sales when they smile during their telephone solicitations. This is true even though the buyer can't see them, because they can hear the smile.

———————— ————————

Smile Science—Who Knew?

You can hear a smile. Scientists from the University of Portsmouth in England found that listeners can identify if a speaker is smiling even when they cannot see the individual. This can produce an unconscious effect on how we interpret the speaker's information. Listeners who were not able to see speakers were able to correctly identify if they were smiling. In addition, the listeners were also able to accurately identify if the speakers were genuinely smiling. (Drahota, et al. 2008)

Smiling and Acknowledgment

If you're feeling generous, you can squeeze every ounce out of your smile. The world's first online juicer has been created to acknowledge your smile. A large fruit juice company, Prigat, is the innovator of the project. The juicer actually works with one small hitch; it will squeeze oranges for you—only if you smile.

The company's theme is, "Open with a smile" and the campaign was developed to strengthen its message by acknowledging your smile. Visitors to the online juicer can smile at the webcam or upload a smiling photo. Once the face recognition technology acknowledges your smile, it actually begins to juice the oranges. The more you smile, the more juice gets squeezed.

Here's the best part. Bottles of fresh juice are donated to charity—compliments of the online smiler, whose donation is digitally acknowledged as well. So far over 20,000 photos have been uploaded and more than 40,000 oranges have been squeezed. That's a whole lot of juice that's been opened with a smile. Think you can put the squeeze on your smile for an ounce or two?

Smile Magic—What's Happening?

People love recognizing and acknowledging the smiles of others. In fact, babies recognize the smile before they can reliably perceive any other facial expression. The more mothers acknowledge their infant's smiles the more socially competent those babies are found to be with their peers in later years. Conversely, depressed mothers who don't smile or acknowledge the smiles of their babies adversely affect their development. These babies are found to become depressed themselves. They smile less, have poorer appetites and sleep less soundly.

Acknowledgment of our smile continues throughout life. Researchers found that jurors gave more lenient sentences when the guilty party was seen sincerely smiling during proceedings. That's because we acknowledge the genuine smile as a sign of trustworthiness, which puts people in a more favorable light—even when we know they have done something wrong.

———————— ————————

Smile Science—Who Knew?

Scientists in the Netherlands found that listeners positively acknowledge others with particular behaviors that include smiling, nodding and maintaining an open body position. The researchers concluded that the smiles and nods of a listener are acknowledgment and signs of agreement and understanding. The lead scientist shared, "By merely smiling or frowning a listener could influence how a speaker reports information and how it is subsequently remembered and possibly passed on. For instance, in witness interrogations, job interviews, politics or psychotherapy, a simple smile or frown could potentially have a large impact." (Beukeboom 2009)

Smiling and Optimism

Nelson Mandela has been described as, "a leader with brains, power, influence and a killer smile." Accredited with negotiating the end of apartheid and becoming the first elected black president of South Africa, he was the recipient of numerous honors, including the Nobel Peace Prize, the Presidential Medal of Freedom and honorary degrees from universities such as Oxford and Harvard. When interviewed on the subject of leadership, the advice that he shared was, "Appearances matter—remember to smile."

When Mandela ran for president of South Africa, his smile became an icon of optimism. Seen everywhere, his election poster was simply a picture of him with his radiant smile. Mandela recognized early on that he was not a great public speaker. As a strategy to catch and keep the attention of audiences, he would do the African Toyi-Toyi dance on the platform while smiling profusely. Displaying this positive emotion, he became an inspiration of hope and optimism for the people of South Africa.

After being imprisoned for 27 years, Mandela could have come across as a tight lipped and bitter individual. Instead, he consciously chose to display a smile, which he described as a "tactical" move to inspire hope. Nelson Mandela's smile became his symbol of forgiveness, triumph and optimism.

Smile Magic—What's Happening?

When a leader has a genuine and joyous smile, sharing it can reinforce his or her charisma. This was the case with Mandela when he did his Toyi-Toyi dance. Mandela's exuberant smile while doing traditional dance moves on the platform was a strategic move. It conveyed to constituents an uplifting sense of optimism during a difficult time. Mandela's actions were able to amplify his spoken message.

Our nonverbal body language and expressions can account

for as much as 75% of the message that people perceive from our communication. Keep in mind that number—most of what influences our judgment does not include any verbal communication. Actions do, in fact, speak louder than words.

People are naturally inclined to look to their leaders for encouragement and positive messages. Because of this, a leader's behavior actually has a strong contagion effect on their followers. Mandela understood this phenomenon and tactically used it. Sharing his genuine smile, Mandela planted a nonverbal message of hope and optimism which helped to support his goals.

———————— ————————

Smile Science—Who Knew?

Scientists at the University of Florida found that charismatic leaders are happier themselves, smile frequently and that they spread their optimism to others. A leader's great smile can also inspire an audience to catch their charisma and make others feel happy. (Erez, et al. 2008)

Smiling and Sound

Scientists have actually been able to prove that saying the long "e" will force a smile and positive feelings. Conversely, when you pronounce the sound of "u" it causes a facial pout and a lousy feeling.

International baby products company, Chicco, is capitalizing on the sound of their company. Pronounced correctly, the company's Italian name is "Kee-ko" and their motto is, "If you say it right, it makes you smile." Chicco is intent on growing their business with an emotionally sound-appealing, multi-million dollar advertising campaign.

Chicco is encouraging parents to submit video clips of their babies saying the company name correctly. The prize is your infant's 15 minutes of fame on Broadway. The baby videos will be displayed on a giant screen 25 stories above Times Square in New York City. Technology captures the video and sends the parents a *keepsake* photo of their smiling baby that they can then post on every social network. Babies everywhere, repeat after me: Kee-ko! Smile and a happy little star is born!

Smile Magic—What's Happening?

How can simply pronouncing a vowel have such a profound effect on our mood? It's because when we say the long "e" in words such as cheese, our facial muscles form a smile. Try it for yourself and say "whee" out loud. When most people do this, the pronunciation of the long "e" will produce a smile. The smile activates a pathway connected to the brain. Feel good chemicals are then released throughout the body. Like magic, we get a happiness boost.

That's why "Say cheese" has become so popular. It is universally repeated before someone takes a photograph. Whether we feel happy or not, it forces a smile, and a happy image is captured. Film Director, Martin Scorsese, has been known to voice his frustration with actors who have had botox injections—and that it's getting difficult to find anyone who hasn't. Some people wind up looking like plastic mannequins. And the depth of their acting can also be affected. When you can no longer move your facial muscles naturally, it changes the messages sent to our brain. The botox is believed to not only diminish lines but also some feelings that are associated with the facial expressions.

So do you smile because you are happy, or do you become happy because you smile? For now, the theory is still up for discussion, but in the meantime you may want to keep smiling and when the need arises, say "cheese"!

———————— ————————

Smile Science—Who Knew?

Scientists at the University of Michigan had participants repeat vowel sounds over and over. The sound of the long "e" consistently induced pleasant feelings, while the short "u" put participants in their worst mood. This supports the theory that it is our facial muscles that influence our mood. (Zajonc, et al. 1989)

Smiling and Play

Nintendo, the manufacturer of Wii Games, provides adults and kids a way to play that spans across generations. Hoping to get people of all ages playing, Nintendo has made some unique contributions to communities around the world. The company has set up thousands of free play and fun stations in senior centers and hospitals. Many times the games help bring seniors and youngsters together. Not only do the seniors find themselves unexpectedly smiling when they play the games, but they discover a fun way to play again with other people of all ages.

Understanding the relationship between play and smiling, Satoru Iwata, the president of the company, said that the whole concept of Wii is, "a machine that makes people smile… getting as many people as possible to show us their smiles when playing a Nintendo game—that's the energy source that drives us."

Smiling and Play

Smile Magic—What's Happening?

Do you remember to smile and take your play seriously every day? If you're like most people, you're play deprived. This is not a healthy scenario. Many adults believe play is just for kids. What comes to your mind when you even hear the word play—smiling children dipping their fingers in brightly colored finger paints? The truth is everyone benefits from playing. It's a fundamental necessity for vibrant and continued brain function. The need to play does not cease just because we grow up.

It is estimated that children smile and laugh around 400 times a day. As adults, the number drops to about 15 times a day. This is a dramatic difference even though, as humans, we are wired to need to play our whole lives. Scientists have found that we are at our happiest when we are engaged in joyful, playful acts that naturally cause us to relax, smile and laugh. They have even found a link between abnormal brain development and play deprivation. At any age, nothing seems to positively fire up brain cells quite like a good play session.

Smile: Happiness Is Right Under Your Nose!

Children don't question their instinctive need to play. They just do it. *Responsible* adults question everything they spend time on that doesn't appear to produce quantifiable results. "The opposite of play is not work but depression." Researchers have found that play is an essential key to living a satisfying and happy life. It also leads to more creative thinking and problem solving.

So how do you play as an adult? You don't need a grandiose plan. Think of an activity that will afford you some sustained pleasure or a burst of laughter or smiling. What brought you joy as a kid? Try to carry that theme into your adult life. Video games like Nintendo's Wii are unique because you can play solo or go social. Pick something that's fun, brings you joy, and makes you smile. Then just do it!

Smile Science—Who Knew?

Scientists found that children laugh and smile more than adults because they play frequently. After studying 1,200 laughing participants, laughter was found to be 30 times more frequent in social rather than solitary situations. This supports the theory that it is easier to smile, when you are alone, than to laugh. (Provine 2000)

Smiling and Simplicity

The happiest people on the planet appear to be in Denmark. For the last 30 years, Denmark has ranked as the number one country in life satisfaction among 178 nations across the planet (the U.S. ranks 23rd). The Danes live in a small country. Their emphasis tends not to be on material possessions. Instead, the Danes typically collect life experiences as life's little treasures.

When I was in college, I had the opportunity to attend the University of Copenhagen in Denmark and live with a Danish family for a semester. Unfortunately, on my way to be an exchange student, the airlines lost my luggage for months. Having very little money, I had to scrounge around for clothes and some essentials. It created a disheartening picture at times. One day my Danish father, Egon, gave me a little plaque to help brighten my spirit. Inscribed on it was: SMIL TIL MIG. Translation: SMILE TO ME.

Smile to me was a common theme in Denmark. The Danes consider the smile a simple pleasure. It can be shared by anyone and at anytime. Smiling is a way to connect with others to create a happy moment in time—a positive little experience in the big picture of life. As I think back on the experience, without question, the smiles of the Danish people are my fondest memory of the trip!

Smile Magic—What's Happening?

What are the factors that social scientists look at to determine happiness? Extrinsic and intrinsic values are very telling when investigating the subject. Extrinsic goals have to do with obtaining things externally such as image, status and money. Intrinsic values have to do with internal factors such as relationships and personal growth. In Denmark there is a great emphasis on intrinsic values.

Caring about others and sharing in a sense of community are strong intrinsic factors that are commonplace in Denmark.

More than 92% of all Danes belong to some type of social club. Also, because of limited space, they have developed housing communities that encourage shared benefits and responsibilities. Their shared smiles are a sign of cooperation that help the Danes connect cohesively to something more important than material possessions.

Having strong intrinsic values, such as an appreciation for simple things in life like a shared smile, make for happy people living happy lives.

Smile Science—Who Knew?

Scientists at Harvard University found that sometimes simple pleasures can produce the greatest happiness. Studies revealed that the receipt of something, as simple as a bouquet of flowers, caused 100% of the recipients to genuinely smile. In addition, the happiness generated by the smile and positive mood transferred from the home, where the flowers were displayed, to the workplace. Recipients of the flowers found themselves smiling more frequently and with more compassion for their fellow workers after receiving the flowers. (Etcoff 2006)

Smiling and Altruism

Smiles are created in Michael Sherwood's trailer. A favorite target of Mother Nature, the trailer has been blown over several times during the last 50 years. Hundreds of people travel on pilgrimage to it every year. They enter with trepidation, but they always leave smiling.

Michael provides free dental services to the poor. He works out of a beat up donated trailer located in Nelson County, Virginia. Michael was retired from a successful dental practice, but felt compelled to help those less fortunate. As a result, he became involved in the charitable dental program.

Michael has restored hundreds of patients' smiles since coming out of retirement. The people he sees cannot thank him enough. Some of them are so poor that they have never even been to a dentist. Michael, grateful for the life he has had, expresses that he is just passing along what he loves best, "giving people back their smiles."

Smile Magic—What's Happening?

Researchers studied the behavior of altruistic individuals and found that they significantly smile more often than non-altruistic individuals. Having a sense of gratitude is a driving force behind their kind behavior.

An altruist's gratitude is frequently reflected in their sincere smiles that they share with others. These genuine smiles also motivate subsequent helping behavior to be passed on to others.

Smile Science—Who Knew?

French scientists found that receiving a genuine smile, even from a stranger, motivates acts of kindness. Researchers studied 800 random supermarket shoppers (half men & half women) between the ages of 20 – 50 years old. Half of the shoppers received a smile from a passing stranger. Those receiving a smile from a stranger were 50 percent more likely to subsequently stop and help another stranger in need. (Guéguen and DeGail 2003)

Smiling and Longevity

Edna Parker is 115 years old and therefore a centenarian. She has been recognized by Guinness World Records to be the oldest woman alive. Friends and family planned a fantastic celebration on her latest birthday. Edna was filled with excitement in anticipation of her party. After all, it's not every day you get to celebrate your birthday. On that special day, she got dressed to the nines in a new polka-dot dress and white shoes.

Amid all the festivities, 115 balloons were released, in her honor, into the azure blue sky over Shelbyville, Indiana. Her birthday party was quite the neighborhood celebration. But when interviewed, people expressed that their best memory of the day was, "Edna's beautiful smile." Through all the hardships endured in her life, Edna has made it a practice to be optimistic and smile. She is not alone. When interviewed, 88% of centenarians expressed that finding something to be grateful for and to smile about, even under difficult situations, is a key factor in staying healthy and optimistic throughout life.

Smile Magic—What's Happening?

We all age, but it is *how* we age that people are most concerned about. There is a growing body of evidence that it is our personality traits and emotions that determine our longevity, health and quality of life as we get older. The Georgia Centenarian Study has been conducted for the last 20 years to identify what factors account for healthy aging and living to be 100 years plus.

At first, genetics were thought to be the primary contributor, but researchers discovered at least 70% of healthy aging is under our control and due to making healthy lifestyle choices. As lead scientist, Peter Martin expressed, "it's personality that turns these things on" and causes healthy lifestyle choices to be made.

Having a positive attitude and learning to express it through positive emotions like smiling leads to optimism. Studies show "optimistic people are healthier. Their biological makeup is different. They have more robust immune systems…they act differently and are more likely to do the things that …are associated with good health." Statistically, optimists live longer and happier lives than pessimists.

Amazingly, the ability to smile frequently has been linked to longevity, better health and overall greater life satisfaction. Our smile directly affects our health. Blood tests reveal that even the anticipation of smiling reduces stress hormones that can compromise our immune system. The smile helps ease anxiety and allows our hearts to work more efficiently. In fact, individuals afflicted with neurological disorders that prevent them from smiling are shown to be more prone to serious depression. People with strong social bonds are also found to live longer, healthier and happier lives. Our smile is a natural innate gift that we use to acknowledge others and show our willingness to cooperate and bond with them.

Smile Science—Who Knew?

Scientists at Wayne State University found that smiling increases life satisfaction, health and longevity. They examined 230 baseball cards of major league players from the official 1952 roster. The researchers determined a smile ratio scale ranging from a big smile, to a partial smile, to no smile. It was found that the players who sported the biggest most authentic smiles in the photos lived 7 years longer than those not smiling. The longevity ranges were: 79.9 years for players with big smiles, 75 years for players with partial smiles and 72.9 years for players with no smiles. The scientists concluded: "Perhaps due to happiness, sociability or conscientious awareness, it has been shown that demonstrating positive emotion, such as smiling, is linked to better health and longevity." (Abel and Kruger 2010)

Smiling and Laughter

Have you ever experienced this scenario? You're sitting in a serious meeting that has been going on for hours. Suddenly, something odd tickles your funny bone. You begin feeling the urge to laugh, but the last thing you want to do is draw attention to yourself.

In an effort to squelch an uncontrollable outburst, you try covering your mouth to hide the smile that is welling up inside you. Despite your best efforts, and to keep your head from exploding—you laugh. Your humorous and cathartic explosion, to your surprise and pleasure, winds up being contagious and soon your colleagues are all letting go of some of their pent up energy and enjoying a good laugh as well.

Smile Magic—What's Happening?

Dogs do it. Even cats and rats do it. And yes people do it too. What is it? They all laugh. Tickle a rat and what does it do? It giggles. Have trouble believing this one? Tune into YouTube and watch scientists as they listen to furry creatures letting loose in uncontrollable, high-pitched laughter. For most mammals, like humans, laughter is a primal and spontaneous function.

Just like smiling, no one has to teach you to laugh. Even deaf people instinctively know how to laugh. Like the smile, it's universal. No matter what language you speak—everyone—everywhere—understands laughter.

Your laugh may sound more like a hee-hee rather than a ha-ha, but no matter the tone or culture, it all means the same thing in the end. When something strikes you funny, your facial muscles form a smile and then you laugh.

We really can't control what makes us genuinely laugh. It's actually an unconscious response. Science does recognize, however, that the infectious quality of laughter is due to its smile factor. Smiles are contagious because of a neurological response and our trait to mirror each other. Our smile is the precursor to laughter and its infectious qualities.

Laughter also has tremendous health benefits. Even just the anticipation of watching a comedy was shown to produce an 87% increase in positive hormones released in our bodies.

Norman Cousins described more than 25 years ago in his book, *Anatomy of an Illness*, that a few minutes of laughter for him would equate to one hour of pain-free sleep. He attributed his beating the odds of his debilitating illness to his self-prescription of laughter. A killer joke really does have killer qualities. Laughter can help destroy tumorous cells and improve cardiovascular blood flow.

Although both pack a powerful health punch, it is easier to smile than to laugh. Have you ever tried to laugh on command—especially if you're alone? It's actually very difficult because the critical stimulus for laughter is another human being. That's why we tend to laugh more watching a funny movie when we are with other people and why laugh tracks are added to sitcoms. We laugh at the sound of other people laughing.

So the next time you feel a good belly laugh coming on—go ahead and reap the benefits. Just remember, you'll have to smile first!

Smile Science—Who Knew?

Scientists in England found that laughter is contagious because the positive sound it produces triggers a response in the same areas of the listener's brain that is activated when we smile. Scientists have known for some time that when we are talking to someone, we often mirror their behavior, mimicking their emotional gestures like their smile or laughter. (Warren, et al. 2006)

Smiling and Inspiration

During her life, Mother Teresa shared, "People are unrealistic, illogical and self-centered, love them anyway…speak tenderly to them. Let there be kindness in your face, in your eyes, in your smile." Known as the *Saint of the Gutters*, Mother Teresa was presented with the Nobel Peace Prize for her lifelong work with the poorest of the poor.

During a train ride from Calcutta, she was inspired to work with the dying and the homeless. Tormented by her own personal pain, she found comfort in the "little things done faithfully and with love." Her smile became a little thing that she shared as an expression of her joy of loving. Attributed with numerous quotes about the smile, Mother Teresa's smile became a symbol of her acknowledgment of the dignity that resides in every human being.

Mother Teresa's genuine smiles have left a legacy of inspiration. The work of this one humble woman has inspired the development of 610 foundations in 123 countries, whose purpose is to help those less fortunate.

Smile Magic—What's Happening?

Mother Teresa did not always feel like smiling, but she understood the value in finding her heartfelt smile to strengthen her dedication and to positively influence others. Her words, "Let's not stop smiling at whomever we meet, especially when it's hard to smile" have left a legacy inspiring millions to help those less fortunate.

Across cultures, genuine smiles produce a ripple effect that generates friendliness, kindness and altruism. The smile has this effect even when it is received from a complete stranger.

Smile Science—Who Knew?

Scientists have found that a shared, genuine smile can create positive effects that can spread and influence altruistic behavior. In studies, it was found that even if a smile is received from a complete stranger, it can still inspire subsequent helping behavior toward others. (Godoy, et al. 2005)

Smiling and Forgiveness

Ralph Waldo Emerson shared, "For every minute you are angry, you lose sixty seconds of happiness." Unfortunately, some people are willing to go to their graves as tight-lipped and angry souls. Wanda Rodriquez, a hospice nurse, is someone who found it in her heart to dig deep to find her heartfelt smile and chose to forgive.

Wanda was assigned to a dying cancer patient. In a remarkable twist of fate, the patient turned out to be her estranged father, whom she had never met. Wanda had been abandoned by her father at birth.

Now, 41 years later, he lay helpless and completely in her care with no other friends or family. Wanda easily could have had a chip on her shoulder. Instead, when interviewed, she expressed her sincere gratitude at finally meeting her father and that it was a true blessing. Their feelings of gratitude for each other were captured on camera and shown by their genuine, loving smiles.

Smile Magic—What's Happening?

Being right isn't always what's right for your body. Harboring anger is like ingesting tiny amounts of arsenic with your morning coffee. It may take awhile, but sooner or later you poison your body and die. People who can't forgive are prone to heart disease and a host of other serious illnesses. Angry people have also been found to smile less than those with a positive disposition.

Are you the type of person who wants everyone to like you? Maybe you go out of your way to avoid drama and confrontation? Unfortunately, life is not fair and it's impossible to please everyone all the time. Despite your best efforts, eventually someone will be angry with you or you with them.

When we ruminate over and over about a bad incident, we become our worst enemy. People who are inclined to short circuit anger are more likely to find it within themselves to smile as a sign of forgiveness. Forgiving is liberating. You are the one who gains the most from the action. People who can forgive are happier and healthier. In a recent Gallup poll, 85% of the responders expressed how important they believed forgiveness to be—yet how difficult they found it to forgive.

So, how can we start the process of forgiveness? You have to first find a way to show yourself some compassion. Recognize that you're human and it's natural to experience angry feelings from time to time in life. The key is to not let your anger control you. Sure, if someone is angry with you they may never find it within themselves to let go and reconcile. You can't change the other person, but you can change your own behavior and perception.

Start the process of forgiveness with finding your heartfelt smile and give it to yourself. In that smile you will begin to experience some peace concerning the situation. This personal peace is the biggest benefit from forgiveness—not necessarily reconciliation with the other person. Your smile is the antidote to the poisonous effects of residual anger and resentment. A heartfelt smile can soothe a troubled soul, especially your own. If you are fortunate enough to patch things up with the other individual, a shared sincere smile can cut through all the crap that can keep us from saying what is really in our hearts.

Smile Science—Who Knew?

Scientists have found when we sincerely share a smile, people feel more comfortable approaching us, as it is perceived as a signal to connect. Also, when spoken words are combined with the appropriate facial expression like the smile, people are more likely to understand the true intent of the message and remember it. (Massaro, et al. 2000)

Smiling and Joy

Amidst the devastation, fear and death caused by the earthquake in Haiti on January 12, 2010, there was one moment of joy. Captured in perhaps the most iconic image of the tragedy and witnessed throughout the world is the photo of little Kiki.

After eight days of inconceivable suffering and fear, Kiki Joachim, a seven year old boy was rescued from tons of rumble and collapsed concrete. The little Haitian boy greeted rescuers with arms outstretched as wide as his joyous smile. When interviewed by reporters about his triumphant expression, Kiki said, "I smiled because I was free—I smiled because I was alive."

Smile Magic—What's Happening?

Do you remember the most joyous moments of your life?

Smiling and Joy

For many, the birth of their child is expressed as their greatest moment of joy—even though it was perhaps also their most painful. The trauma of giving birth has been likened to passing a bowling ball through a keyhole. And yet, it is nearly impossible not to joyfully smile at the birth of a child. In that moment, when you see your baby and smile—you do not feel your pain. The endorphins produced when you smile act as a natural painkiller.

And then there's the joy from seeing your baby's first smiles. Scientists from Baylor College of Medicine have learned that the joy you experience from seeing a baby smile activates the pleasure receptors of the brain. Researchers have found that the smile provides the mother with a neurological surge that prompts her to want to take care of her child.

Some scientists believe that a baby's first smiles mark the beginnings of a sophisticated form of communication that has played a role in our development. Months after birth, babies begin to share feelings of joy and happiness which initiates their bonding process with others. How does the baby do this? They may look at something that makes them happy like a toy and then look at another person while maintaining that joyous smile. The shared smile is a baby's way of making an emotional connection and an invitation to interact. Daniel Messinger, a lead scientist in this field stated, "I take smiling to be a social signal. I really think that babies are learning what joy is by sharing it with someone else."

Then there are the studies that indicate we can change our mood because our brain doesn't differentiate between that which is real or pretense. Many studies show that by simply modulating our facial muscles to force a smile we can enhance a mood and experience the physiological and psychological benefits of that expression. As a result, even fake smiles provide huge benefits to the person forcing the smile and can bring about a more joyful mood.

So are we smiling because we are joyous or are we joyous because we smile? This is a mystery that has baffled scientists for centuries. Consider the case of little Kiki in Haiti. At first, Kiki expressed fear and recoiled as he was being pulled from the rubble and saw all the strange faces. It was only when he saw the smiling face of his Aunt, who called his name, that he became overjoyed, outstretched his arms and smiled.

Smile Science—Who Knew?

Smiles are powerful expressions of joy. It is almost impossible not to smile when we see a joyous smile because of its contagion factor. Scientists at Duke University determined that because the smile activates the orbital frontal cortex, the reward center of the brain, we like and more easily approach those people who smile at us. Smiles are such an important communication signal that we can spot them at a greater distance than any other facial expression—as much as 300 feet away, the length of a football field. (Gladstone and Parker 2002)

Smiling and Near Death Experience

Patrick Tierney was declared a flatliner. While suffering cardiac arrest, he had no brain activity and was pronounced clinically dead. During the medical rush to revive him, he had a near death experience.

In his transcendence, Patrick found himself in what he describes as "a form of heaven." He was within a beautiful landscape, instantly calmed and soothed by a translucent light. His deceased parents were smiling broadly at him.

Patrick was resuscitated. His vision of his parents' smiles and the beauty of the whole experience had left him with no fear of death. Today, Patrick expresses that he smiles more frequently and shares, "If dying is anything like the experience I had, then it's not a problem."

Smile Magic—What's Happening?

Based on a Gallup poll, at least 10 million Americans have admitted to having had a near death experience.

It doesn't matter if you consider a near death experience to be delusional episodes or the consciousness continuing after clinical death, they do have common characteristics. These frequently include an out-of-body sensation, a bright light and a calming and welcoming image, that is often exhibiting a beautiful smile.

Smile Science—Who Knew?

Scientists studied more than 3,500 cases of near death experience. Some studies revealed that no matter what the nationality, age, culture or religion of the patient, key features are common in a near death experience. This often includes an image of a deceased relative or parent with a welcoming smile. In addition, the patient may become euphoric after the episode, smiling more frequently with greater appreciation and joy for life. (Parnia, et al. 2001)

Smiling and Death

In 1948, Cicely Saunders met a young Polish man, David Tasma, who was dying of inoperable cancer. Tasma had escaped the Warsaw ghetto and was lying alone in a London hospital where Saunders was a social worker. Tasma's pain, loneliness and anguish had a profound effect on her which led to a revelation. Saunders wanted to find a way to provide a means for a "final smile and support to those dying alone." As a result, she became the founder of the first hospice organization to provide compassionate care for the dying.

Saunders' vision, "led to a model that has changed the face of dying across the world." There are currently 3,200 hospices in the U.S. alone, and 8,000 hospices in 100 countries around the world. Approximately 1 in every 3 Americans will receive hospice care at the end of life. As expressed by a hospice agency, their goal is to help patients die with dignity and to show that there is always something new to be experienced. "Sometimes that something new—is simply a final shared smile."

Smile Magic—What's Happening?

Receiving a smile from someone who is dying is a gift that can open your heart to give beyond your limits. Shared silent smiles can cut through negative emotions and feelings that can poison our last words. A smile shared at death is a means to silently communicate acceptance, gratitude and love.

We come into this world hardwired and ready to smile. No one has to teach us to smile. For many, the smile is their last gift of genuine kindness that they share—naturally.

Picture yourself at death. What are you smiling about?

Smile Science—Who Knew?

Even in our grief, the smile is construed as an invitation to approach and connect. Scientists found that when we are mourning, if the bereaved can somehow find the means to occasionally smile at loved ones, it will encourage them to approach you during this difficult time. Seeing the smile helps friends and family to feel less helpless and more inclined to stay close to you, which helps lift the sorrow a bit. Interestingly, mourners that can show occasional sincere smiles during their initial grief period, do much better in their recovery months and even years later than those who did not smile. (Bonanno and Keltner 1997)

NOTES

Smiling and Purpose
1. Carnegie, Dale. 1936. How to Win Friends & Influence People, revised edition (1981) New York: Simon & Shuster.
2. Lewis, M.B. & A. J. Edmonds. 2005. "Searching for Faces in Scrambled Scenes." Visual Cognition, Vol.12, pages 1309-1336.

Smiling and Birth
3. Hrdy, Sarah Blaffer. 2009 Mothers and Others: The Evolutionary Origins of Understanding. Cambridge, MA: Harvard University Press.

Smiling and Cooperation
4. Jamison, Josiah. U.S. Paralympic team. http://www.teamusa.org/Athletes/JA/Josiah-Jamison.
5. Matsumoto, David and Bob Willingham. 2009. "Spontaneous Facial Expressions of Emotion of Congenitally and Non-Congenitally Blind Individuals." Journal of Personality and Social Psychology, Vol.96(1), pages 1-10.

Smiling and Bonding
6. Iacoboni, Marco, John C. Mazziotta, Jennifer H. Pfeifer, and Mirella Dapretto. 2008. "Mirroring Others' Emotions Relates to empathy and Interpersonal Competence in Children." NeuroImage, Vol.39(2008), pages 2076-2085.

Smiling and Health
7. May is for Miracles: Chico's FAS, Inc. Is Committed to Making a Difference in

NOTES

Children's Lives - One Miracle at a Time;Chico's Fashion Press Release April, 18, 2013. http://www.chicosfas.com/phoenix.zhtml?c=72638&p=irol-ewsArticle&ID=1808120&highlight=

8. Ong, Anthony D., Daniel K. Mroczek, and Catherine Riffin. 2011. "The Health Significance of Positive Emotions in Adulthood and Later Life." Social and Personality Psychology Compass, Vol.5(8), pages 538-551.

Smiling and Diet

9. Unilever's Smile-Activated Ice Cream Machine: http://www.psfk.com/2010/06/unilevers-smile-activated-ice-cream-machine.html

10. Dingemans, Alexandra E., Carolien Martijn, Anita T. M. Jansen and Eric F. van Furth. 2009. "The Effect of Suppressing Negative Emotions on Eating Behavior in Binge Eating Disorder." Appetite, Vol.52(2009), pages 51-57.

11. Martijn, Carolien, Marlies Vanderlinden, Anne Roefs and Jorg Huijding. 2010. "Increasing Body Satisfaction of Body Concerned Women Through Evaluative Conditioning Using Social Stimuli." Health Psychology,Vol.29(5), pages 514–520.

Smiling and Luck

12. Wiseman, Richard. 2003. "The Luck Factor." SKEPTICAL INQUIRER The Magazine For Science And Reason, Vol.27(3), May/June 2003: http://richardwiseman.files.wordpress.com/2011/09/the_luck_factor.pdf

13. Wiseman, Richard. 2003.The Luck Factor: Changing Your Luck, Changing Your Life: The Four Essential Principles, New York: Hyperion.

Smiling and Perception

14. Ten Facts about Washington's Teeth: http://www.mountvernon.org/george-washington/teeth

15. Voth, Lori, 2007. "Dialectical Behavior Therapy DBT Skill: Smile When Your Are Sad":http://voices.yahoo.com/dialectical-behavior-therapy-dbt-skill-smile-when-404570.html

16. Soussignan, Robert. 2002 "Duchenne smile, emotional experience, and autonomic reactivity: A test of the facial feedback hypothesis." Emotion, Vol.2(1), Mar 2002, pages 52-74.

Smiling and Symbolism

17. Harvey Ball World Smile Foundation and World Smile Day: http://www.worldsmileday.com/
18. Berridge, Kent C. and Piotr Winkielman. 2003. "What is an Unconscious Emotion? (The Case for Unconscious 'Liking')", Cognition and Emotion, Vol.17 (2), pages 181-211.

Smiling and Memory

19. Tsukiura, Takashi and Roberto Cabeza. 2008. "Orbitofrontal and Hippocampal Contributions to Memory for Face-name Associations: The Rewarding Power of a Smile." Neuropsychologia, Vol.46(9), pages 2310–2319.
20. Tsukiura, Takashi and Roberto Cabeza. 2011. "Remembering Beauty: Roles of Orbitofrontal and Hippocampal Regions in Successful Memory Encoding of Attractive Faces." NeuroImage, Vol.54(1), pages 653-660.

Smiling and Inner Peace

21. Eat, Pray, Love, a 2010 film produced by Plan B Entertainment and distributed by Columbia Pictures. Based on the 2006 memoir by Elizabeth Gilbert, Eat, Pray, Love: One Woman's Search for Everything across Italy, India and Indonesia, London: Penguin Books, Ltd.
22. Zeidan, Fadel, Katherine T. Martucci, Robert A. Kraft, Nakia S. Gordon, John G. McHaffie, and Robert C. Coghill. 2011. "Brain Mechanisms Supporting the Modulation of Pain by Mindfulness Meditation." The Journal of Neuroscience, Vol.31(14): pages 5540-5548.

Smiling and Endurance

23. Garfield, Charles A. Ph.D. with Hal Zina Bennett. 1984. Peak Performance: Men-

tal Training Techniques of the World's Greatest Athletes, Los Angeles: Tarcher.
24. Kraft, Tara L. and Sarah D. Pressman. 2012. "Grin and Bear It: The Influence of Manipulated Facial Expression on the Stress Response." Psychological Science, Vol.23(11), pages 1372-1378.

Smiling and First Impressions

25. Ekman, Paul. 2001. "Smiling" in C. Blakemore & S. Jennett (Eds) Oxford Companion to the Body, London: Oxford University Press.
26. Ekman, Paul. 2003. Emotions Revealed: Recognizing Faces and Feelings to Improve Communications and Emotional Life, New York: Henry Holt and Company, LLC.

Smiling and Productivity

27. Zappos.com makes Fortune's list of best places to work:/www.vegasinc.com/news/2013/jan/17/zapposcom-makes-fortunes-list-best-places-work/
28. Chafkin, Max. "The Zappos Way of Managing", Inc., May, 1, 2009: http://www.inc.com/magazine/20090501/the-zappos-way-of-managing.html
29. Salemi, Vicki. 2010. "Start Smiling: It Pays to be Happy at Work" August 14, 2010, Forbes.com
30. Pryce-Jones, Jessica. 2010. Happiness at Work, Maximizing Your Psychological Capital for Success, West Sussex, UK: Wiley Blackwell.

Smiling and Beauty

31. Wrigley Press Release. 2009. "Face Facts: Smiles More Attractive than Makeup", May 18, 2009: http://www.wrigley.com/uk/press/news-releases-print.aspx?id=1382
32. O'Doherty, J., J. Winston, Hugo D. Critchley, David I. Perrett, D. Mike Burt, and R. J. Dolan. 2003. "Beauty in a Smile: The Role of Medial Orbitofrontal Cortex in Facial Attractiveness." Neuropsychologia, Vol.41, pages 147-155.

Smiling and Rejection

33. Duell, Mark. 2011. "Sorry you didn't get the job, Dad, that's so funny: Hilarious

video of the baby who laughed hysterically as dad tore up rejection letter.": http://www.dailymail.co.uk/news/article-1361850/YouTube-video-baby-Micah-laughing-father-Marcus-McArthur-tears-rejection-letter.html#ixzz2czL8PETU

34. DeWall, C. Nathan, Jon K. Maner, and D. Aaron Rouby. 2009. "Social Exclusion and Early-Stage Interpersonal Perception: Selective Attention to Signs of Acceptance." Journal of Personality and Social Psychology, Vol.96(4), pages 729-741.

Smiling and Intimacy

35. Mass R., M. Hölldorfer, B. Moll, R. Bauer, and K. Wolf. 2009. "Why We Haven't Died Out Yet: Changes In Women's Mimic Reactions to Visual Erotic Stimuli During Their Menstrual Cycles." Hormones and Behavior, Vol.55(2), pages 267-271.

Smiling and Animals

36. Kids and Ponies – Molly's Foundation: http://mollythepony.com/Home_Page.html

37. Nagasawa, Miho, Kensuke Murai, Kazutaka Mogi and Takefumi Kikusui. 2011. "Dogs Can Discriminate Human Smiling Faces from Blank Expressions." Animal Cognition, Vol.14(4), pages 525-533.

Smiling and Depression

38. VanSwearingen, Jessie M., JeffreyF. Cohn and A. Bajaj-Luthra. 1999. "Specific Impairment of Smiling Increases the Severity of Depressive Symptoms in Patients with Facial Neuromuscular Disorders." Aesthetic Plastic Surgery, Vol.23(6), pages 416-423.

39. Van Swearingen, Jessie M. and Jeffrey F. Cohn. 2005. "Depression, smiling and facial paralysis." in The Facial Palsies: Complementary Approaches, C. H. G. Beurskens (Ed.), pages 373–386. Utrecht: Lemma Publishing.

Smiling and Business

40. Get happy!! Japanese workers face smile scanner: http://www.theguardian.com/money/blog/2009/jul/07/japanese-smile-scanning

41. Kober, J. Jeff. 2009. The Wonderful World of Customer Service at Disney, Performance Journeys Publishing

42. Pugh, S. Douglas. 2001. "Service with a Smile: Emotional Contagion in the Service Encounter." Academy of Management Journal, Vol.44(5), pages 1018-1027.

Smiling and Social Networking

43. Naumann, Laura P., Simine Vazire, Peter J. Rentfrow, and Samuel D. Gosling. 2009. "Judgments of Personality Based on Physical Appearance." Personality and Social Psychology Bulletin, Vol.35(12), pages 1661-1671.

Smiling and Judgment

44. Chang, Anita. 2008. "Beijing Olympic Hostesses Practice Poise", USA Today, January 9, 2008: http://usatoday30.usatoday.com/news/world/2008-01-09-1042503909_x.htm

45. O'Doherty, John P., J. Winston, Hugo D. Critchley, David I. Perrett, D. Mike Burt, and R. J. Dolan. 2003. "Beauty in a Smile: The Role of Medial Orbitofrontal Cortex in Facial Attractiveness." Neuropsychologia, Vol.41(2), pages 147-155.

Smiling and Advertising

46. Wasserman, Todd. 2011. "Kraft Mac & Cheese Launches 'Smile Tagging', Partners With Cheezburger":http://mashable.com/2011/07/13/kraft-smile-tagging-cheezburger/

47. Tomkovick, Chuck, Rama Yelkur, Ashley Hofer, Clay Theiler, and Daniel Rozumalski. 2010 "Super Bowl Ad Likeability in the New Millenium.", in 2010 Spring Conference Proceedings Published by Marketing Management Association, page 43:http://www.youtube.com/watch?v=-GHAO-3HCFU

Smiling and Renewable Resources

48. Guinness World Record Largest Smiley Face: http://www.rabwah.net/world-largest-smiley-face-guinness-world-record/

49. Art of Living Foundation Smile Campaign: http://ru.artofliving.org/smile-mi-

ami-campaign-captures-pearly-whites-camera
50. Fredrickson, Barbara.2009.Positivity: Groundbreaking Research Reveals How to Embrace the Hidden Strength of Positive Emotions, Overcome Negativity, and Thrive. New York: Crown Publishers.

Smiling and Culture

51. Singapore's Champion a Smile Campaign, "Smile When You See the Mirror": http://news.xin.msn.com/en/singapore/article.aspx?cp-documentid=4257851
52. Marsh Abigail A., Hillary A. Elfenbein and Nalini Ambady. 2007. "Separated by a Common Language: Nonverbal Accents and Cultural Stereotypes About Americans and Australians." Journal of Cross-Cultural Psychology, Vol.38(3), pages 284-301.

Smiling and Contagion

53. Jell-O Pudding Face Mood Meter:http://www.thedenveregotist.com/news/local/2011/july/29/jello-pudding-face-mood-meter-comes-outdoor
54. Dimburg, Ulf, Monika Thunberg, and Kurt Elmehed. 2000. "Unconscious Facial Reactions to Emotional Facial Expressions." Psychological ScienceVol.11 (1), pages 86-89.

Smiling and Loneliness

55. Fear of Lonliness: http://www.readersdigest.ca/magazine/around-world-one-question-whats-your-greatest-fear
56. Lander, Karen and Sofie Metcalfe. 2007. "The Influence of Positive and Negative Facial Expressions on Face Familiarity." Memory, Vol.15(1), pages 63-69.

Smiling and Competence

57. Abel, Millicent H. and H. Watters. 2005. "Attributions of Guilt and Punishment as Functions of Physical Attractiveness and Smiling."The Journal of Social Psychology,Vol.145(6), pages 687-702.

NOTES

Smiling and Thought Control
58. Fredrickson, Barbara. 2009.Positivity: Groundbreaking Research Reveals How to Embrace the Hidden Strength of Positive Emotions, Overcome Negativity, and Thrive. New York: Crown Publishers.

Smiling and Relationships
59. Buelhman, Kim T., John M. Gottman and Lynn F. Katz. 1992. "How a Couple Views Their Past Predicts Their Future: Predicting Divorce from an Oral History Interview", Journal of Family Psychology, 5(3-4), pages 295-318.
60. Hertenstein, Matthew J., Carrie A. Hansel, Alissa M. Butts, and Sarah N. Hile. 2009. "Smile Intensity in Photographs Predicts Divorce Later in Life." Motivation & Emotion, Vol.33, pages 99-105.

Smiling and Self-Esteem
61. Smile Pinki, 2008 Oscar winning documentary movie:http://en.wikipedia.org/wiki/Smile_Pinki
62. National Smile Month and Dr. Nigel Carter: http://www.walesonline.co.uk/news/health/knowing-whats-lurking-your-toothbrush-2031031
63. Harker, L. A. and D. Keltner. (2001) "Expressions of Positive Emotion in Women's College Yearbook Pictures and Their Relationship to Personality and Life Outcomes Across Adulthood." Journal of Personality and Social Psychology, 2001, Vol. 80, No. 1, 112-124 DOI: 10.1037//0022-3514.80.1.112
64. Marcus, J. R. (2008) "'Smile Doctors' Create, Restore and Enhance Patients' Smiles." Science Daily (Oct. 8, 2008)http://www.sciencedaily.com/releases/2008/10/081008114416.htm
65. Martijn, Carolien, Marlies Vanderlinden, Anne Roefs and Jorg Huijding. 2010. "Increasing Body Satisfaction of Body Concerned Women Through Evaluative Conditioning Using Social Stimuli." Health Psychology, Vol.29(5), pages 514–520.

Smiling and Education

66. Goldberg, Carey. 2006. "Harvard's Crowded Course to Happiness 'Positive Psychology' Draws Students in Droves." The Boston Globe, March 10, 2006.
67. Seligman, Dr. Martin:http://www.authentichappiness.sas.upenn.edu/default.aspx
68. Ben-Shahar, Tal and Achor, Shawn. "Positive Psychology: The Science of Happiness". Harvard University:http://camsolivia.hubpages.com/hub/The-Most-Popular-Class-at-Harvard-University-Positive-Psychology-The-Science-of-Happiness

Smiling and Creativity

69. Bataclan, Bren. Smile Art Project:http://www.bataclan.com/
70. Nadler, Ruby T., Rahel Rabi and John Paul Minda. 2010. "Better Mood and Better Performance: Learning Rule Described Categories Is Enhanced by Positive Mood." Psychological Science, Vol.21(12), pages 1770-1776.

Smiling and Income

71. Julia Roberts ad for Lavazza's A Modo Mio coffee: http://theflorencenewspaper.com/new/julia-roberts-paid-1-6-million-for-italian-coffee-commercial/
72. Shore, Danielle M. and Erin A. Heerey. 2011. "The Value of Genuine and Polite Smiles.", Emotion, Vol.11(1), pages 169-174. http://www.theguardian.com/education/2011/may/10/economic-value-smile-research

Smiling and Technology

73. Bélisle, Jean-Francois and Bodur H. Onur.2010. "Perception of Consumers Based on Their Avatars in Virtual Worlds", Psychology & Marketing, Vol. 27(8), pages 741–765.
74. M.I.T. Media Lab and Autism Research:http://www.feelguide.com/2011/03/03/donating-your-webcam-smile-to-mits-autism-research-will-also-lead-to-emotion-reading-computers/
75. Baccus, Jodene R., Mark W. Baldwin and Dominic J. Packer. 2004. "Increasing

NOTES

Implicit Self-Esteem through Classical Conditioning." Psychological Science, Vol.15(7), pages 498-502.

Smiling and Attitude

76. Blanchflower, David G. and Andrew J. Oswald. 2008. "Is Well-being U-Shaped over the Life Cycle?", Social Science & Medicine, Vol.66(8), Pages 1733-1749:
77. Wiseman, Richard. 2009. "The Science of Happiness": http://richardwiseman.com/happiness

Smiling and Leadership

78. Rath, Tom and Barry Conchie. 2008.Strengths Based Leadership: Great Leaders, Teams, and Why People Follow.New York: Gallup Press.
79. Bono, Joyce E. and Remus Ilies. 2006. "Charisma, Positive Emotions and Mood Contagion."The Leadership Quarterly, Vol.17(4), pages 317-334.

Smiling and Listening

80. Napoli, Lisa. 2010. "Weed-Whacking Goats Will Work For Food", National Public Radio, July 9, 2010:http://www.npr.org/templates/story/story.php?storyId=128411947
81. Drahota, Amy, Alan Costall and Vasudevi Reddy. 2008. "The Vocal Communication of Different Kinds of Smile." Speech Communication,Vol.50(4), pages 278-287.

Smiling and Acknowledgment

82. Prigat's "Open with a Smile" campaign developed a User Generated Orange Juice application that integrated the real world with the virtual one, December 2010:http://www.prigat.com/News_And_Events.html
83. Beukeboom, Camiel J. 2009. "When Words Feel Right: How Affective Expressions of Listeners Change a Speaker's Language Use." European Journal of Social Psychology, 39 (5), pages 747-756.

Smiling and Optimism

84. Stengel, Richard. "8 Leadership Lessons from Nelson Mandela", Time Magazine, July 9, 2008: http://www.time.com/time/world/article/0,8599,1821467-1,00.html http://www.google.com/url?sa=t&rct=j&q=&esrc=s&frm=1&source=web&cd=2&ved=0CC8QFjAB&url=http%3A%2F%2Fwww.ymresourcer.com%2Fdocuments%2F8_Leadership_Lessons_From_Nelson_Mandela.doc&ei=umAqUvDalYjA4AOljlDoDg&usg=AFQjCNF6qpYAKoxGiaei-k5-RaY27pv1xQ

85. Erez, Amir, Vilmos F. Misangyi, Diane E. Johnson, Marcie A. LePine and Kent C. Halverson. 2008. "Stirring the Hearts of Followers: Charismatic Leadership as the Transferal of Affect." Journal of Applied Psychology, Vol.93(3), pages 602-615.

Smiling and Sound

86. Chicco Launches Digital Interactive Campaign on Times Square Billboard with Aerva Technology:http://aerva.com/chicco-campaign-launches-with-aerva/#.Uir6rqjD_IU

87. Zajonc, R. B., Sheila T. Murphy and Marita Inglehart. 1989. "Feeling and Facial Efference: Implications of the Vascular Theory of Emotion. Psychological Review, Vol. 96(3), pages 395-416.

Smiling and Play

88. Gantayat, Anoop, "Iwata is Super Positive." IGN Entertainment, January 18, 2008: http://www.ign.com/articles/2008/01/19/iwata-is-super-positive

89. Provine, Robert. 2000. "The Science of Laughter: Far from mere reactions to jokes, hoots and hollers are serious business: They're innate -- and important -- social tools." Psychology Today, November 1, 2000.

Smiling and Simplicity

90. Buettner, Dan. 2010. "Lessons from Denmark" Thrive: Finding Happiness the Blue Zones Way, Washington D.C.: National Geographic Society:http://www.bluezones.com/2012/02/lessons-from-denmark/

NOTES

91. Etcoff, Nancy. 2006. "New Behavioral Research Demonstrates Flowers in the Home Make a Positive Impact on Our Lives.":http://community.passiongrowers.com/wp-content/uploads/2010/08/flowersinthehome1017061.pdf

Smiling and Altruism

92. Nelson Co. Dentist Making People Smile: http://thegoodmuse.com/wordpress/wp-content/uploads/2013/03/Raegan-Readers-Digest-Article.pdf, http://www.youtube.com/watch?v=-ENndIIj5Lo

93. Guéguen, Nicolas and Marie Agnes De Gail. 2003."The Effect of Smiling on Helping Behavior: Smiling and Good Samaritan Behavior." Communication Reports, Vol.16(2), pages 133-140.

Smiling and Longevity

94. Edna Parker celebrates 115th birthday:http://www.worldrecordacademy.com/human/oldest_person_world_record_set_by_Edna_Parker_80215.htm

95. Abel, Ernest L. and Michael L. Kruger. 2010. "Smile Intensity in Photographs Predicts Longevity." Psychological Science, Vol.21(4),pages 542-544.

Smiling and Laughter

96. Cousins, Norman. 1979.Anatomy of an Illness, 1979, New York: W. W. Norton & Company, Inc.

97. Warren, Jane E., Disa A. Sauter, Frank Eisner, Jade Wiland, M. Alexander Dresner, Richard J. S. Wise, Stuart Rosen and Sophie K. Scott. 2006. "Positive Emotions Preferentially Engage an Auditory–Motor-'Mirror' System."The Journal of Neuroscience, Vol,26(50), pages 13067–13075.

Smiling and Inspiration

98. Quotes from Mother Teresa: http://www.motherteresaquote.com.

99. Godoy, Ricardo, Victoria Reyes-García, Tomás Huanca, Susan Tanner, William R. Leonard, Thomas McDade, and Vincent Vadez. 2005. "Do Smiles Have a Face Value? Panel Evidence from Amazonian Indians." Journal of Economic Psychology,

Vol.26(4), pages 469–490.

Smiling and Forgiveness

100. O'Shaughnessy, Patrice, 2010. "Terminal cancer patient reunited with long lost daughter, who turns out to be hospice nurse", New York Daily News, September 3, 2010:

http://www.nydailynews.com/new-york/terminal-cancer-patient-reunited-long-lost-daughter-turns-hospice-nurse-article-1.438072#ixzz2eFSY2aCW

101. Gorsuch, Richard L. & Hao, J. Y. 1993. "Forgiveness: An exploratory factor analysis and its relationship to religious variables", Review of Religious Research, Vol.34(4), pages 351-363.

102. Massaro, Dominic W., Michael M. Cohen, Jonas Beskow and Ronald A. Cole. 2000. "Developing and Evaluating Conversational Agents" in Embodied Conversational Agents, Justine Cassel, Ed., Cambridge, MA: MIT Press, pages 287-318.

Smiling and Joy

103. Hazelton, Liz, "Haiti earthquake miracle boy Kiki: 'I smiled because I was alive... but now I'm sad for my dead brothers and sister'", Daily Mail, January 23, 2010:

http://www.dailymail.co.uk/news/article-1245216/Haiti-earthquake-miracle-boy-Kiki-describes-moment-plucked-rubble.html#ixzz2eFV65H2N

104. Day, Nicholas, "Why Do Babies Smile?", Slate.com, July 1, 2010:http://www.slate.com/articles/double_x/doublex/2010/07/why_do_babies_smile.html

105. Gladstone, Gemma L., and Gordon B. Parker. 2002. "When You're Smiling, Does the Whole World Smile for You?" Australasian Psychiatry, Vol.10(2), pages 144-146.

Smiling and Near Death Experience

106. Gallup, George, Jr. with William Proctor. 1982.Adventures in Immortality: A Look Beyond the Threshold of Death, New York: McGraw-Hill:http://www.unex-

plainedstuff.com/Afterlife-Mysteries/Individual-Human-Experience-with-Death-and-the-Afterlife-Near-death-experiences-ndes.html

107. Parnia, Sam, D.G. Waller, R. Yeates and Peter Fenwick. 2001. "A Qualitative and Quantitative Study of the Incidence, Features and Aetiology of Near Death Experiences in Cardiac Arrest Survivors." Resuscitation, Vol. 48(2), pages 149–156.

108. Parnia, S. and Peter Fenwick. 2002. "Near Death Experiences in Cardiac Arrest: Visions of a Dying Brain or Visions of a New Science of Consciousness." ResuscitationVol.52(1), pages 5–11.

109. Parnia Sam, K. Spearpoint and Peter B. Fenwick. 2007. "Near Death experiences, Cognitive Function and Psychological Outcomes of Surviving Cardiac Arrest.", Resuscitation,Vol.74(2), pages 215-221.

Smiling and Death

110. Smith, Wesley, J., "Dame Cecily Saunders; The mother of modern hospice care passes on." The Weekly Standard, July 19, 2005: http://www.weeklystandard.com/Content/Public/Articles/000/000/005/846ozowf.asp: http://en.wikipedia.org/wiki/CicelySaunders

111. Bonanno, George A. and Dacher Keltner. 1997. "Facial Expressions of Emotion and the Course of Conjucal Bereavement." Journal of Abnormal Psychology, Vol.106(197), pages 126-137.

General

112. LaFrance, Marianne, (2011) Lip Service, Smiles in life, death, trust, lies, work, memory, sex and politics, W.W. Norton & Company, New York

113. Star, Elan Sun, (2006), Smile! The Secret Science of Smiling, Roaring Lion Publishing, Inc., Asheville, NC

114. Davis, S. F., and J. J. Palladino. (2000). Psychology (3rd ed.). Upper Saddle River, NJ: Prentice-Hall, Inc.

For Chucky with everlasting gratitude, love and smiles.

Acknowledgments

It is with deep gratitude that I would like to thank Henric Gomes for his patience, support, kindness and commitment to this project. I would also like to thank Brenda and Lynn Griebahn for their sincere enthusiasm, feedback and continued support of me, particularly through all the draft changes. Many thanks also to Eva Sugden Gomez, Linda Christina Beauregard, Diane Loveless, Doug Crites, Lori Foehr, Tom McCabe, Roy Gravener, Wil Christiansen, Barbara Errickson-Connor, John Connor, Glen Stanford, Roman Gomez, Randy Simmons, Karen T. Bartlett, and Peter Miskech. Your insight and feedback will always be appreciated and invaluable. A special thank you to Ann Stillwell and Camille Laz who kept my creative perspective on the right track. Many smiles to all of you.

About the Author

Mary Anne Puleio, Ph.D., is an award-winning professional speaker, author and artist. Her work in the information industry has been with entrepreneurs, universities, and international organizations. Grateful for her life opportunities, she founded Smile Up, LLC. Mary Anne resides in Columbus, Ohio and Naples, Florida where she is also the Director of USA Dance, the national non-profit ballroom association.

Books by the author include:
- *Remarkable Smile Secrets*
- *Smile Up Inspirations*
- *Smile: Happiness Is Right Under Your Nose!*

For information about presentations, literature and products
Visit the author's website at: www.smileup.org

Other Books in the Smile Up Series

Remarkable Smile Secrets

Bite-sized smile tips filled with scientific revelations and heart-warming original art. This book is guaranteed to be instantly enlightening and to make you smile! Presented in full color.
to order books please go to www.smileup.org

Coming Soon

Smile Up Inspirations

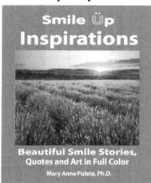

Fearless Smiles

Made in the USA
Middletown, DE
19 September 2018